THE
EVERYTHING™
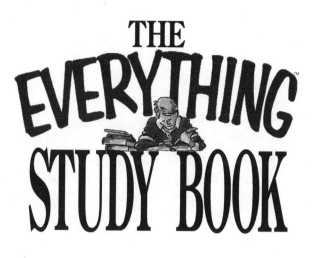
STUDY BOOK

The *Everything*™ Series:

THE EVERYTHING BARTENDER'S BOOK
THE EVERYTHING CHRISTMAS BOOK
THE EVERYTHING WEDDING BOOK
THE EVERYTHING STUDY BOOK

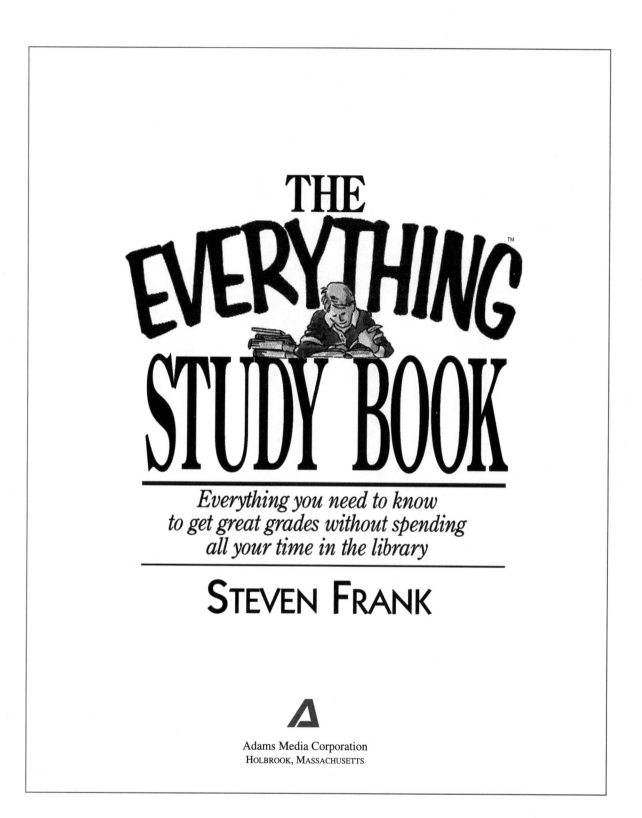

THE
EVERYTHING™
STUDY BOOK

Everything you need to know
to get great grades without spending
all your time in the library

STEVEN FRANK

Adams Media Corporation
HOLBROOK, MASSACHUSETTS

An Everything™ Series Book.
The Everything™ Series is a trademark of
Adams Media Corporation.

Published by Adams Media Corporation
260 Center Street, Holbrook, MA 02343

ISBN: 1-55850-615-2
Printed in the United States of America.

First Edition
J I H G F E D C B A

Library of Congress Cataloging-in-Publication Data

Frank, Steven, 1967–
    The everything study book / Steven Frank.
        p.   cm.
    Includes index.
    ISBN 1-55850-615-2 (pb)
    1. Study skills.   I. Title
LB1049.F63   1996
371.3′028′12—dc20
                                                                                        96-15094
                                                                                              CIP

This publication is designed to provide accurate and authoritative information with regard to the subject matter covered. It is sold with the understanding that the publisher is not engaged in rendering legal, accounting, or other professional advice. If legal advice or other expert assistance is required, the services of a competent professional person should be sought.
        —From a *Declaration of Principles*, jointly adopted by a Committee of the American Bar Association and
        a Committee of Publishers and Associations

This book is available at quantity discounts for bulk purchases.
For information, call 1-800-872-5627
(in Massachusetts, 617-767-8100).

Visit our home page at http://www.adamsmedia.com

TABLE OF CONTENTS

CHAPTER 3: READING TEXTS

CHAPTER 4: WRITING ESSAYS

CHAPTER 5: TAKING TESTS

CHAPTER 6: SECRETS OF STUDY SUCCESS

PREFACE

When I was a sophomore in college, I pulled an all-nighter to study for a midterm examination on Shakespeare. This was my typical way of studying. I spent the entire night reading over my notes and things I'd underlined in the textbook. With the help of a dozen cups of coffee, I managed to stay up all night, although by 3 a.m. I was practically climbing the walls.

The next day in class, I was thrilled to see that the two essay questions were relatively easy. They involved plays that I knew really well. I did an adequate job on the first essay, but something terrible happened on the second one: Exhaustion hit me as hard as if I'd been knocked over by a hard-covered edition of *The Complete Works of Shakespeare*. I knew what I wanted to write, but I just didn't have the energy to write out the whole essay. I managed to scribble some ideas, but I was too tired support them with details. Even though there was plenty of time to finish the essay, I turned in my exam booklet and went home to get some sleep.

Later, after I'd napped and was again thinking like a rational human being, I got angry at myself. I knew the answer to that question and could have written a dynamite essay. But, because of the way I'd spent the night studying, I had inadvertently

sabotaged myself. I would have been better off, I realized, not having studied at all than staying up all night. There had to be a better way to study.

Over the course of the rest of my education, as both an undergraduate and graduate student, I experimented with various strategies and techniques for studying more effectively and efficiently. The strategies included in this book are the ones I found to be most successful. Many of these I learned the hard way, through plain old trial and error. Others, though, I learned by talking to people who were themselves highly successful students.

While I have spent many years as a student, I have also been a teacher, and gained insight into the teacher's point of view of the educational process. I now have a much more accurate sense of the kinds of things that impress teachers most on exams and essays. As you'll see, being a successful student involves establishing a clear line of communication with your teacher, which is greatly improved by maintaining an understanding of your teacher's own aims and perspectives.

I am extremely pleased to be able to share these strategies and insights with you. But let me emphasize what is probably the most important thing I've learned, as both teacher and student, about the educational process. I've found that learning can be a boring, stressful, and ultimately useless process, or it can be one of the most exciting and personally enriching experiences of your life. What you get

out of it depends on what you put into it.

Making the effort to be a good student is well worth it—and not just because you improve your chances of getting high grades. It would be naive to deny the importance of getting high grades, as a great deal in your immediate future depends on your grades, from receiving scholarships to getting into graduate schools to finding employment. But, in the long term, grades have little impact on the outcome of your life. However, the skills you develop while you are a student—things like how to approach a problem strategically and intelligently, how to communicate clearly and efficiently with others, and how to apply what you know to new situations—can be useful your entire life.

CHAPTER 1

The Path to Study Success

The Genius

When he was two years old, the Genius was given an IQ test and his score topped the charts. By the age of ten, he was proving complex geometric theorems and conversing in Latin. When he goes to college (only as a formality—he needs a diploma to get a job), the work is a cinch. With his photographic memory, he never needs to take notes during lectures; it all comes back to him instantly, without any effort. He also never has trouble understanding anything, so he never has to ask for help. During exams, he laughs to himself at how easy the questions are, and he is always the first person to finish. Of course, he receives straight A's.

The Workaholic

The Workaholic reads everything assigned by the professor not once or twice but five times. She attends each and every class, even if she is so sick she can barely move, and she writes down every word the professor says. At home, she rewrites the notes meticulously, in different colors in three separate notebooks. She spends her "free" time in the library, reading her notes over and over again. She takes the entire semester to research and write an essay, and her professors are always impressed by the enormous number of sources she includes in her bibliography. Before exams, she refuses to eat or sleep so she can spend twenty-four hours a day studying. She is happy to find that she does receive A's in her courses—even if she didn't have time to go to movies, or make friends, or participate in extracurricular activities.

To hear these stories, you'd think that high grades only go to the super-smart or the super-human workers. Sure, some people are naturally gifted and don't have to work all that hard, but they make up only a small percentage of the population. Others manage to get good grades without the benefit of an astoundingly high IQ, and they don't necessarily spend every minute of every day poring over the books, sacrificing their social lives and personal happiness. So, if it's not a question of innate intelligence or being willing to work day and night, what is the secret of school success?

The answer is having the right study skills. Regardless of what you study, the *way* you study can make the difference between an A and an F. And the good news is that these skills can be learned. Just as people aren't born knowing how to hit a baseball or play the piano, you can *develop* the skills that will enable you to learn new material and truly understand it.

No one is born knowing how to study. Unfortunately, there isn't nearly as much opportunity to learn how to study as there is to play baseball or the piano. Everyone assumes students will somehow figure out how they are supposed to study. Some, through trial and error, are able to develop the skills that make them successful; others need more guidance.

WHAT THIS BOOK WILL DO

The Everything Study Book addresses all the basic skills that comprise studying—reading texts, taking notes, writing essays, preparing for and taking exams—and outlines methods and techniques that will help you to become a much more efficient student. As you'll see throughout the book, the way you approach these tasks can make all the difference.

Each chapter outlines a step-by-step approach to a particular study task that makes developing study skills as easy as following a recipe. You'll also find detailed examples that illustrate these strategies in action. You won't just know what the strategy is; you'll also understand why it works. As a result, you'll be able to adapt these strategies to meet your specific goals.

This book can be used by anyone who wants to improve their study skills and try to raise their grades. It can be particularly helpful for students in their first years of college, when the stakes are raised and you have to study much more than you have before—unless you develop study skills pretty

quickly then, you're in for a rough time. However, the skills in this book can also be used by high school students who want to improve their performance for their current classes while gaining skills to prepare them for the college-level work that awaits them.

GENERAL THEMES

Many of the strategies outlined in this book involve tracking the general themes of various subjects. You'll find as your studies progress that certain ideas come up again and again, both within single courses as well as throughout your education. Keeping track of these themes and incorporating them into your overall knowledge is a vital part of the learning process.

Tools of the Trade: A Student's Shopping List

The following items are essential tools of the trade for any student. Make certain you have them at the start of the school year—chances are you'll need most of them!

- Required textbooks and course materials (such as course packets)
- Notebooks and paper
- Folders with pockets (for collecting handouts in class)
- Pens (blue or black ink)
- Pencils, eraser, and pencil sharpener
- A typewriter or computer (if you don't want to purchase one, make certain you have access to one)
- Typing or computer paper
- Stationery and envelopes
- Diskettes (for computer use)
- A desk calendar or schedule/assignment book
- A wall calendar
- Reference guides (such as a dictionary and thesaurus)
- A backpack, bookbag, or briefcase
- Wite-Out (for correcting mistakes when proofreading)
- A stapler and staples
- Paper clips
- Index cards (3" x 5")
- A tape recorder/portable cassette recorder
- An alarm clock and wrist watch
- Specialty items: Depending on the courses you take, you might also need a compass, calculator, graph paper, lab report sheets, slide rule, protractor, scissors, paste, markers, highlighters, and so on.

KEEPING YOUR EYE ON THE BIG PICTURE

One of the major techniques discussed in this book is keeping the big picture in mind as you study. It's all too easy to become so caught up in the details that you lose sight of what you are studying and why. Without a sense of this big picture, you can easily feel unfocused; however, if you maintain a clear sense of what you are doing and why, you are more likely to remain on track.

It is also important to maintain a sense of the big picture throughout your education. You can become so involved in the intricacies of specific classes, assignments, and requirements that you forget what you're doing it all for in the first place.

Your "big picture" is a personal one, and it can be different from everyone else's. The important thing is that you remain aware of what your big picture is. Throughout your studies, as you become immersed in the details of various subjects and tasks, make certain that you step back every so often to appreciate that big picture. Try to see how each task you go about fits into it. If you see how each task contributes something of use to you personally, you'll remain much more focused on your work; you'll also find your studies more fulfilling.

You can maintain sight of the big picture by setting goals for yourself. For each task, you should set a short-

term goal, such as reading a chapter of a textbook thoroughly or studying for an upcoming exam. At the same time, though, you should set larger goals for your entire education and understand that all of the short-term goals help you get closer to the big one.

To determine a goal, consider your purpose in attending school. If the only reason is because your parents said you must, you are not going to be very happy. There must be something you hope to gain in your studies, and it doesn't necessarily have to be the same thing your parents or teachers want. You may, for example, want to develop specific skills to help you in a certain career. Or, you might want to receive high grades so you can get into the graduate school of your choice. There might be more personal factors involved as well, such as the desire to better yourself, to become a more educated person, and to experience new ways of thinking and seeing.

PASSIVE VERSUS ACTIVE STUDYING

Although they don't realize it, many students approach studying as a *passive* activity. They think that as long as they look at their notes and read their textbooks they are covering the material adequately. Studying, in this sense, is not much different from watching television: You simply look, listen, and somehow "take it all in." But you probably are never going to have an exam on a particular television show.

The material you study in school, though, is different; you *will* be tested on it, and you need to recall information in great detail. Moreover, you will often need to take information you've learned and apply it to other areas. Sitting back and "taking it all in" is therefore not going to cut it.

Rather than approaching studying in this passive manner, this book repeatedly emphasizes the importance of *active* study. Active studying means you *do* something. Instead of merely looking at and listening to new material, you *think* about it and, in the process, make it a part of your general knowledge. As a result, you are better able to remember the information for exams and also to apply it to other situations.

You'll find that all the strategies in the book include methods to involve you actively in your studies. In a general sense, though, you need to establish yourself as an active student right from the start. That means acknowledging that your education involves work—hard work. Even though you might be sitting at a desk or lying on the couch reading over notes, your mind must remain hard at work. As soon as you slip into a passive mode, the material before you will be lost and you might as well have been watching television.

COMMUNICATION IS THE KEY

When people think about education, they tend to view it as centering on teaching and learning. However, for both students and teachers, the essence of school is communication. Information is communicated to you by teachers and through textbooks. You, in turn, are expected to communicate back to professors (and sometimes peers) your understanding of the material through exams, papers, and presentations.

If you've ever traveled to a foreign country, you know how difficult it can be to communicate with someone who speaks a different language. While it poses a challenge, the language barrier is also one of the things that makes traveling so exciting, as you work to understand things and in turn to make yourself understood.

Communication in school can also be very difficult. The language is somewhat different from the language you are used to speaking. Professors speak differently from your friends, while textbooks and other academic resources are written in a unique style. Not only the new vocabulary of the new information but also the way it is presented will seem strange.

In this book, you'll learn how to become a better student by becoming better at communication in the academic world. In the first half of the book, we'll concentrate on translating the information being communicated to you—in classroom lectures and textbooks—into a language you understand. In the second half, we'll concentrate on the other route—communicating it all back to the professor on exams and in papers.

I Learned It at the Movies

Just as you can learn something from almost anything you read, you can often learn things by watching a movie. However, you do need to watch with a careful eye. Movies take liberties with the subject matter—even movies that claim to portray historical events. And you should never watch a movie adaptation of a literary work rather than reading it, as movie-makers often change the original versions. If you answer questions on an exam based only on seeing the movie without having read the original text, you'll probably get a great deal wrong. Worse, your professor will know you took the lazy way out. But if you keep the limitations of movies in mind while you watch, you can still learn something.

The movies on this list are based on real or historical events. While they do take liberties with the subject matter, these movies convey an overall view of events and their outcome, as well as a general sense of life in particular times and places. Having that picture in mind while you study or read can help make the subject matter more accessible to you.

All the President's Men
Apollo 13
Farewell My Concubine
Gandhi
Guilty By Suspicion
JFK
The Last Emperor
Lawrence of Arabia
Little Big Man
Malcolm X

Mississippi Burning
Nixon
Passage to India
Quiz Show
Ragtime
The Right Stuff
Roger and Me
Schindler's List
The Thin Blue Line

Throughout all of this, we'll concentrate on how you communicate to yourself. While teachers and books might impart information, it will be meaningless unless you understand for yourself what you are learning. Studying, as you'll see, is a matter of engaging in a constant dialogue with yourself, during which you ask yourself questions, attempt to answer them, and then ask more questions.

You should feel good to know that you can learn how to communicate better, just as you can learn to play baseball or the piano better. That means you can learn how to be a more efficient, more successful student. And you don't need to be a genius or workaholic to do it.

Important Points to Remember

1. Always keep sight of the big picture; remember why you are in school and what you hope to gain.

2. Set short-term and long-term goals for yourself.

3. Be an active student, not a passive one.

4. Think of studying as communicating—with teachers, texts, fellow students, and yourself.

CHAPTER 2

Taking Notes

Three Note-Taking Nightmares

Lightning Liz

Liz's strategy for taking classroom notes is simple: Write down every single word the professor says. If you sit behind her in class, you'll see her hand flying across her notebook in a blur. For a class lasting an hour, she takes sixty or seventy pages of notes; by the end of the semester, her notebook is roughly the size of Webster's Dictionary. When she gets home each night after a day of classes, her hand has swollen to about the size of a mango. But, as she soaks her throbbing wrist in a bucket of ice, she smiles, knowing that she has gotten the entire day's lectures down in her notebook. At least, that's what she thinks. When it comes time to prepare for the final, she hires a football player to pull all of her notebooks to the library. By the day of the exam, she's only been able to memorize the first notebook, which covers only the first three weeks of class. Unfortunately, the exam is on the entire semester.

Casual Calvin

Calvin takes his seat in class, puts his feet up on the chair in front of him, and folds his hands comfortably behind his head, in a pose somewhat like a model's in an underwear ad. His strategy is to just sit back, relax, and soak in the professor's words. He says that if he doesn't worry about writing, he can simply absorb the material and then use his photographic memory to recall it later. At the end of the class, he does indeed remember the general themes of the lecture. When the final exam comes six weeks later, he sits down to write his essay. He clearly remembers learning about, say, the basic principles of psychology, but he's a bit foggy on the exact terms. He struggles to remember: "There's the, what was it? The ego, the, um, something like ego. Oh, yeah, the superstar ego. And that other thing. What was it? The Kid? The Bid? Oh, yeah, the Sid." Throughout his essay, he refers to the basic psychological drive known as the "Sid" instead of the correct term, the "id." Even though much of his essay is well written, his professor is so appalled by his use of the terms "superstar ego" and "the Sid" that he gives him an F.

Symbol Simon

Realizing it takes way too much time and effort to write down every word, Symbol Simon has developed a complicated sign system for his notes. He has special pictures, abbreviations, and symbols for every word; as new terms come up, he continues to add to his repertoire. His notes are much more concise this way, taking up only one or two pages. At the end of the semester, when it comes time for him to study, he sits down with his notes and tries to read them. This is akin to deciphering hieroglyphics, especially since he has trouble remembering what some of his original signs mean. After sweating and working away at the difficult passages, he manages to come up with a sketchy translation of his own notes. Of course, the exam is going to begin in a few hours and he has not yet actually studied the notes.

These are obviously exaggerations that show how ill-advised these note-taking strategies are. But, believe it or not, most students adopt some form of one of these, without thinking about the trouble they are creating for themselves in the very way they take notes.

The crucial mistake all three have made, a mistake common to most students, is that they have neglected to communicate to themselves. Their sole concern has been to take down or take in what the teacher has said. They have failed, though, to do so in a way that makes sense to themselves.

When it comes time to study for exams, all three have far more work ahead of them than is necessary. They've made the mistake of taking notes they don't really understand, which means they have to work just as hard figuring out the notes as they did taking them.

LIVE AND IN PERSON

The point of taking notes is not to have a copy of what the teacher has told you. If that were the case, why would there be lectures at all? Wouldn't it just be easier to read it in a book? The fact is that live communication is very powerful and very effective. For example, if you were to have a telephone conversation with someone who speaks Swahili, it would be almost impossible for you to understand what he was saying (unless, of course, you happen to speak it yourself). However, if you were to have the conversation in person, you'd probably understand something. You'd be able to read body language, watch gestures, and pay attention to facial expressions, which provide information about what is being communicated. In turn, the speaker would see from your expression what you do and do not understand and adopt other techniques to try to communicate.

By attending live lectures, you can gain a deeper understanding of the material being presented. As in a conversation with someone who speaks another language, you'll receive additional information through body language, expression, and tone of voice. Also, simply by being present and listening attentively, you'll pick up more of the material than you would by merely reading. Live performance, after all, is generally more compelling and likely to hold your interest; that's why people pay so much for concert and theater tickets.

In this chapter, we're going to learn a method for taking effective lecture notes. We'll learn how to take notes that capture the important points covered by the professor or class instructor. We'll also learn how to write those notes in language you can understand, which will also help you learn the material. Following this method will make it much easier for you to study for exams because you'll already have done much of the tough work—listening.

Be a Packrat—You Never Know What You'll Need Again

Many students are so relieved when the semester is over they throw away all their notes. That's a serious mistake. You've worked hard taking those notes. And, more importantly, you never know when you might need to refer back to them.

Many of the courses you take will interconnect, particularly those within your major or concentration. As you move on to more advanced levels, you'll find you need to refer to notes from earlier courses to refresh your memory about certain key points.

You also may take courses that seem completely unrelated to one another, only to find that some point or issue will come up that you have previously addressed. For example, you may be reading a novel in an English class that refers to specific historical events. If you've taken a history class about that period, you can read your notes and get more information about those events, which in turn can help you understand the novel. Imagine how impressed your teacher will be if, in class discussion, you can provide some of that background information.

At the end of the semester, rather than throwing away all your notes, neatly label and put them someplace safe and accessible. Consider purchasing a file cabinet to store them in. If you've been using a loose-leaf notebook (as recommended in this book), you can take the pages out of the binder and put them in a folder. That way you can reuse the binder next semester. Just make certain you label the folder with the course title and year. A file cabinet will help keep everything organized.

In addition to saving old notes, consider holding onto some of your required textbooks and other course materials. It's tempting at the end of the semester to sell all your books back to the bookstore—especially given how expensive books are these days. However, if there is any chance you will refer to a book—particularly if it was used in a course that is part of your major—it is probably worthwhile to hold onto it. One option is to sell only the textbooks and hold onto all other books. Textbooks tend to be more expensive than other books, and you get back a significant amount of money. Other books often bring only a fraction of the original cost (especially if they are paperbacks). If you sell one of these but wind up having to purchase it again, you actually lose rather than save money!

IT BEGINS BEFORE YOU PUT PEN TO PAPER

Taking effective notes doesn't start when you begin writing; it begins with being an effective *listener*. We take it for granted that we all know how to listen, that listening is a natural skill requiring no work at all. The truth is, listening is a difficult task and very few people know how to do it well. Have you ever been in the midst of a conversation with someone, nodding your head in agreement, and suddenly found yourself unable to respond to a question they've just asked? While you may have heard him, you weren't listening to him.

Why is listening so difficult? One reason is that we confuse *hearing* with *listening*. Hearing is *passive*; it means some sound has reverberated in your ear, whether or not you want it to, and there's been a noise. Listening, on the other hand, is an *active* process. It implies that you must *do* something to accomplish it. It takes action and, often, work to listen well. For example, let's say you are sitting on a crowded train talking with a friend. You hear the noise of the train, the chatter of passengers around you, the boom box being blasted by a teenager and, somewhere in all that, you even hear your friend. But to understand what your friend is telling you, you need to *do* something; you need to listen to distinguish her words from all the background noise.

The same principle applies to classroom lectures. There may not be the same amount of noise in a lecture room as on a crowded train (although there is plenty of distracting racket, from feet shuffling to heaters blowing), but you still have to work hard to listen to the professor's words.

Here are some strategies for effective listening. They can help with your note-taking as well as with any interpersonal encounters, from conversations to job interviews. Develop good listening skills now and they'll last a lifetime and continue to bring you success. People respect someone who listens carefully. More importantly, those who listen are certain to catch important information that others don't.

STRATEGIES FOR EFFECTIVE LISTENING

1. Make the Effort

The first step to effective listening is to realize that listening takes effort. It won't happen on its own and it's not something that is going to take place naturally, just by your being there. Go into situations where it's important for you to listen determined to listen, and listen carefully. Concentrate. It may be difficult at first, but in time you'll get better.

2. Pay Attention to the Speaker

It is very difficult to listen to someone if you are not giving all your attention to that person. Ideally, you should look at the person's face the entire time she is speaking. However, in a lecture this is not always possible because you also need to look at your notes from time to time. Try, if you can, to write while keeping your eye on the professor. This may make your notes more messy than usual but, in time, you'll get more adept at writing without looking at the page. If you can't write and look at the professor at the same time, make certain to look up from your notes frequently. This will ensure that you are maintaining a direct line of communication with her.

If the professor is explaining a difficult concept, you are much better off not writing and looking only at her. This way, you can concentrate on listening and understanding. After the professor is finished, jot down a few notes or phrases to help you remember what was said.

3. *Minimize Distraction*

To maintain that direct line of communication between you and the speaker, it's important to minimize all outside distractions. Different things can be distracting. Perhaps there's someone very attractive who you always sit near in class and who occupies more of your attention than the professor. Maybe a friend you sit with can't resist chatting during the lecture. Even something as tame as chewing gum or a grumbling stomach can begin to sound like a major earthquake when you are trying to pay attention to something else. Choose your seat carefully and come to class prepared to listen and well fed.

You might also decide to sit closer to the professor if it helps you concentrate better. Sitting in the first few rows is not absolutely crucial; in fact, some people feel very uncomfortable being that close to the professor. However, if you are having trouble hearing or concentrating, try sitting in the first or second row. You might be surprised at how much more of the lecture you catch.

Additionally, the way you sit can also affect your ability to pay attention. If you slouch in the chair, your eyes won't be focused on the speaker. Each time you want to look at the teacher, you will have to lift up your entire head, and the effort needed to do that can disrupt your note-taking. Instead, it is much more effective to sit with your back against the chair back. Place the sheet of paper in the center of the desk and hold it in place with whichever hand you do not use to write. If you sit in this position, you should be able to watch the professor while writing; you also will be able to glance down at your notes by just moving your eyes, not your entire head.

4. *Watch for Lapses*

Become more attuned to the times when your mind is drifting to other subjects or your eyes are wandering out the window. When this happens, focus your attention back on the speaker immediately. Be aware that everyone is prone to lapses in attention, and that if you can recognize when your mind wanders, you will begin to correct yourself much faster and not miss as much.

5. *Work at It*

Listening, like any skill, improves as you work at it. As you try to concentrate in different situations, you'll find you get better and better at it.

6. Watch for Clues from the Speaker

Listening effectively means more than paying attention to the words of the speaker. People convey a great deal of information through the way they speak as well as what they say. Get in the habit of concentrating on additional signals from a speaker besides spoken words. Pay attention to the speaker's tone of voice, the volume of their speech, pauses, hand gestures, and body language—these signals can enhance your understanding of the speaker's words. Additionally, by being alert to these elements in addition to spoken words, you have more to occupy your attention, ensuring that you remain actively engaged in the lecture, conversation, or discussion.

By the Way, You Should Leave the Tape Recorder at Home

Some students think they'll take the easy way out by bringing a tape recorder to class, and relying on that instead of taking notes. However, the tape recorder ultimately means much more work than they realize. The students get home and have all that tape to sit through, which means, in effect, going to class twice.

By taking notes in class instead, you're already beginning to digest and to edit the information. For example, you might not write down information that you already know or have taken notes on previously. You also don't need to write down the detailed explanations your professor makes to recall and understand a particular concept. Since your notes are succinct, they will take far less time to read over than it would take to listen to an entire lecture on tape again.

Then there's the problem of mechanical difficulties. Tape recorders are machines. What if the batteries run out or the tape doesn't record well and you can't hear what the teacher said? What if the tape gets eaten? Minimize these risks by leaving the tape recorder at home.

There is one way that a tape recorder may help you. If you must miss a lecture for some reason, you might want to have a friend record it so you'll be able to keep up. Make certain, though, that you listen to the lecture and take notes just as if you were sitting in class. It's also a good idea to do this before the next class so you can keep up with the course.

Effective Note-Taking

The Paper

If you go to the stationery shop or bookstore, you'll see hundreds of types of supplies, from legal pads to spiral notebooks to high-tech notebook "systems" that promise to do everything from keeping a time schedule to programming a VCR.

The best way to keep notes, though, is on loose-leaf paper (that's the kind with three holes that you can put in and take out of a notebook). There are several reasons why this is recommended. For one thing, you won't have to lug your entire notebook to class. You can simply keep some loose-leaf paper in a folder or small binder that you carry throughout the day to all your classes. When you get home, you can then transfer the relevant sheets into your permanent binder(s). You can either keep separate binders for different subjects or one big binder with different subjects separated by dividers.

By not carrying all your notebooks with you, you not only save your back muscles, but you also buy yourself insurance. There's always the danger that you'll lose or misplace a notebook at some point and, if you're really unlucky, it will happen late in the semester, when it will be tough to make up the lost material. If you lose a folder containing just that day's notes, it's not so traumatic.

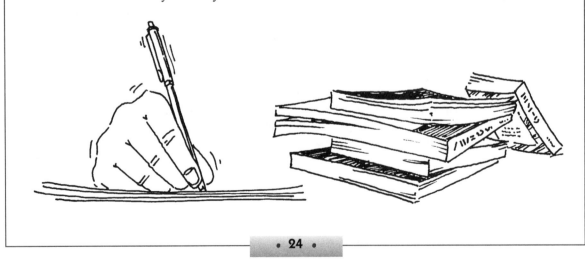

Loose-leaf paper also enables you to move sheets around in the binders. You can add additional notes, rewrite notes, or shift things around without much difficulty. As we'll see, this flexibility will help you take notes that are more accurate and that better prepare you for exams.

THE PEN

You should really select a decent ball-point pen to write with. Pencils may seem like a good idea because you can erase and change things with them; however, pencils break and wear down, leaving you to sharpen them in the midst of class. Pencil is also harder to read than ink, so write with a pen! You can always cross stuff out if it's incorrect. Just avoid those inky, fine-point pens that leave smudges all over the paper, not to mention your hands.

Some students like to take notes with different-colored pens or highlighters. For example, they might put key terms and phrases in one color, and the definitions of those terms in another. Doing this helps some people retain information more effectively when they study. However, taking notes in different colors is time-consuming, and therefore not recommended. While attending class, you should remain focused on the teacher, not on color-coding your notes. If you would like to color-code your notes, wait until you are out of class and have more time. But don't feel you have to color-code your notes in order to study efficiently; as you'll see, the strategies outlined in this book provide you with a number of ways of retaining information, without having to spend time juggling your pens.

A NOTE ON LAPTOP COMPUTERS

Some people have begun to bring laptop computers to class. While this might seem like a good idea, it's not really recommended for several reasons. For one thing, most people write by hand more quickly than they type. Also, typing on a laptop can distract your fellow students and, worse, your instructor. More importantly, writing by hand gives you greater flexibility. For example, you can jump back to previous notes to make relevant additions. You can also draw signs, and use arrows and symbols more easily by hand. As we'll soon see, you'll be working a great deal with the notes you take in class, making additions and revisions. It's easier to do this on paper than on the computer.

If you want to keep your notes on your computer, you can always type them when you get home. In fact, this process is a good way to help you rethink and reorganize your notes, and it will help you remember them.

STRATEGIES FOR EFFECTIVE NOTE-TAKING

We're about to go through a step-by-step strategy for taking more effective notes. This strategy has two stages: The first takes place during a class, the second outside the classroom. Most students think they are finished with their notes the minute class ends. But that's wrong.

The strategy outlined below involves beginning your notes in class and finishing them later on. This method will relieve a lot of the pressure if you think you have to get down everything during a lecture. There's another major benefit to following this strategy: The extra attention you devote outside of the classroom guarantees you understand your own notes. This means that when exam time comes around, you won't have to panic because you don't remember—or worse, don't understand—things you learned earlier in the semester.

Stage One: In Class

1. Make preparations
2. Write down all key terms
3. Include brief definitions and explanations of key terms (wherever possible)
4. Construct a rough outline
5. Note general themes of the lecture

Stage Two: Note-Taking Outside Class

1. Read over your notes
2. Ask yourself questions
3. Make notes on your notes
4. Go to other sources
5. Additional sources of information
6. Fill in more information
7. Rewrite your notes (optional)

STAGE ONE: TAKING NOTES IN CLASS

1. Make Preparations

It's smart to get to class a few minutes early. For one thing, you'll be able to choose your seat. More seriously, though, coming in late can distract and offend the teacher, and it's never a good idea to get the professor angry. It's also difficult to begin work if you rush to class, arriving out of breath and flustered, with your thoughts on the outside world. By coming early, you can relax and decompress for a few minutes and put yourself in the right frame of mind. If you have time, you might want to look over your notes from the previous class to help set your attention on the day's subject matter.

When you get to class, take out a new sheet of paper. You may have brought the notes from the previous class with you, but you should always start each class with a fresh piece of paper. This is because lectures tend to have their own separate topics or themes. By keeping separate notes, you can better identify distinct themes.

Always put the date and subject at the top of the first sheet, so you can put them in the proper binder or section at home. Next, you should draw a line down the page about three inches from the left, so that you have an extra-wide margin (most pieces of notebook paper already have about a one and a half inch margin). Your paper will then look like this:

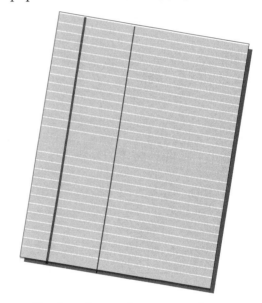

During class, take notes only on the right side of the margin. Leave the left side totally blank—you'll be using that space when you get to stage two, working on notes at home. You should also take notes on only one side of the paper; the back side will be used later.

Make certain you have plenty of paper on hand throughout the lecture. Always put the date and subject on the top of each sheet; that way, if sheets from different days and classes get mixed up, you'll be able to figure out where they go. And for each new sheet, continue drawing that line and taking notes only on the right side.

2. *Write Down All Key Terms*

The first and foremost commandment of note-taking is this: You cannot write down everything the professor says. This is so important that it bears repeating: *You are not going to be able to write down everything the professor says!*

And what's more, if you try to write down everything the professor says, you'll find yourself in deep trouble. At some point, no matter how fast you can write, you will miss something. Either you won't hear clearly, or you'll become distracted, or your hand will cramp up. And then, if you're like many students, you'll panic. As you struggle to figure out what you missed, you'll miss even more. And before you know it, you won't have notes for the bulk of the lecture.

So let's make it clear right from the beginning. *You don't have to write down everything.* Your next question probably is, "So what exactly am I supposed to write down?" In order to answer that question, we need to examine the purpose of taking notes.

In taking notes, your aim should not be to create an exact transcript of the professor's lecture. If that were the case, the professor would simply hand out photocopies. A great deal of what you hear in class might be familiar to you and, therefore, doesn't really need to be recorded. Writing down information and concepts that are new and unfamiliar should be your priority.

During lectures, the main thing professors do is communicate new information. The majority of it is specific, such as names of people or places, significant dates, certain theories, formulas, and concepts. These are the *key terms* of the lecture.

Most often, these terms are going to be new to you, which makes them harder to remember. A goal of note-taking, then, is to keep track of all these key terms.

Your professor might often write down key terms on the board. You should *always* note anything the teacher writes on the board. But there will also be many other terms that the professor might not write—if these are new to you, make certain you write them down as well.

By the way, there's a strong chance these terms will appear in the reading assigned for the class. If you complete the reading before class, the terms will ring a bell when they come up in the lecture. Keeping up with required reading can help a great deal when you take notes as you will feel somewhat familiar with the material. Later, we'll be talking more about the way in which reading and lectures come together and how both sources help you prepare for tests.

As you take down these key terms in class, don't worry about their correct spelling or pronunciation. Just write out words the way they sound. Try to be as accurate as you can be. Later on, you can find out the right way to spell them.

Believe it or not, if you write down just these key terms, you'll have a pretty accurate representation of the entire lecture. These terms are most often the points around which the entire lecture is based. You can be certain that if you showed your professor this list of terms, she would be able to recreate the lecture for you in its entirety. Can you?

You might be surprised how much you actually remember, merely by seeing key terms. As long as you've been listening carefully, these terms can serve as triggers that help you recall much of what you heard in the lecture. Of course, you might not remember everything about each term, but chances are you can remember *something* about most of them.

Sample Lecture and Key Terms
Following is a passage from a typical lecture, followed by a list of key terms you might include in your notes. As an exercise, try reading the lecture yourself and creating your own list of key terms. How do they compare to the key terms included here? You can also test yourself to see how much of the passage you recall just by reading over the list of key terms.

Considered by many to be the founder of modern psychoanalysis, Sigmund Freud continues to be one of the most influential, albeit controversial, figures in psychology. Living and working in turn-of-the-century Vienna, Freud revolutionized the way in which we think of the human personality and how it is shaped and developed, not to mention the ways in which we examine our own dreams.

Among his many highly influential theories was his model of human personality. Freud conceived of personality as constructed of three distinct but conflicting entities: the *id*, *ego*, and *superego*. The id consists of the most basic biological drives and urges that we know from birth, including those for food, drink, physical comfort, and sexual pleasure. For this reason, Freud described the id according to the pleasure principle; that is, as the desire for instant pleasure and gratification, no matter the cost. As an infant grows, it begins to understand that the urges of the id have to be in accord with the actual circumstances of the external world. The ego then develops to satisfy the urges of the id within the workings of the real world. Rather than obey the pleasure principle, the ego adheres to the reality principle. As a child matures, it begins to internalize the morals, values, and rules set by parents and society, and in turn the superego develops. The superego is the internal judge of behavior, deeming what is good or bad, moral or immoral. It is the conscience.

Here's another way to think of the model for personality. The ego represents a person's actual, day-to-day behavior in society, the face one presents to the outside world. The id and the superego are both factors trying to influence the ego; the id pushes the ego to pursue pleasurable urges, while the superego enforces judgments, advocating "correct" behavior and warning about punishments for incorrect behavior. According to Freud, these forces are often waged in internal, subconscious conflict that can create anxiety. One way to cure anxiety is to identify the internal conflicts that cause it.

Anxiety, Freud said, is often associated with the urges we experience as children but quickly learn are forbidden, usually when we are punished for attempting to act on them. In order to try to get rid of the anxiety, a child tries to get rid of the forbidden urge; this is known as repression, because the child pushes the thought out of its conscious deep into the subconscious, far from the face presented to the outside world. However, the forbidden urge continues to break through to the surface, sometimes throughout our lives, which can create anxiety.

To grapple with the anxiety created when the forbidden urges resurface, people create psychological defenses, which Freud called *defense mechanisms* that protect the ego from the urges of the id. An example of a defense mechanism is *projection*, the attribution of forbidden urges to someone else (for example, instead of thinking you hate your parents, you might think your sister hates them) and *denial*, the refusal to acknowledge the urge whatsoever, even if it means completely ignoring aspects of reality (when you basically think, "No way José! Not me!").

Freud attempted to apply this theory of unconscious conflict to areas of everyday life. One example is his theory of dreams, presented in *The Interpretation of Dreams*, written in 1900. Freud said that dreams are efforts at *wish fulfillment*; they depict the gratification of the urges of the id, without the controls of the ego and superego. An example Freud often referred to was a painting called "The Prisoner's Dream," which depicts in simple terms the prisoner receiving his wish fulfillment in his dreams—his escape from jail.

However, since the forbidden urges can still create anxiety, even in dreams, they do not usually appear in such simple form; instead they are translated into images that disguise their actual meaning. Freud distinguishes between the *latent dream*, which represents the actual desires of the dreamer, and the *manifest dream*, which the dreamer actually experiences in which the latent desires are presented in disguised form. Very often the manifest dream makes use of symbolism, relying on images that actually stand for something else. For example, Freud believed that dreaming of water or horses carries erotic meanings. Freud claimed that analyzing the symbols in dreams was a means of uncovering and curing the patient's anxieties.

This aspect of Freud is one of the more controversial and contested. Various studies have been conducted on patient's dreams, and they have failed to find consistent systems of dream symbols that apply to a single dreamer, let alone to many dreamers. Water and horses in my dream may mean something quite different in yours. Still, there is no ignoring how influential Freud's writings on dreams have been, not only in psychology, but also in art, music, and literature.

KEY TERMS

founder of modern psychoanalysis

Sigmund Freud

turn-of-the-century Vienna

model of human personality

id

ego

superego

pleasure principle

reality principle

subconscious conflict

anxiety

repression

defense mechanisms

projection

denial

theory of dreams

The Interpretation of Dreams (1900)

wish fulfillment

"The Prisoner's Dream"

latent dream

manifest dream

3. Include Brief Definitions and Explanations of Key Terms

Write brief explanations or definitions of the key terms next to them, whenever possible. Again, don't write down everything the professor says. Try to jot down just a few words or phrases that will help you remember what a term means later on.

If you can't write much about a particular term, don't worry. *Just keep listening and writing!* You'll have plenty of time to fill in more information later. If your professor has moved on to introduce a new topic or key term while you are still taking notes on a previous one, then leave that term behind.

You don't need to write perfect, grammatically correct sentences. These notes are written only for you; as long as they make sense to you, nothing else really matters.

DEVELOPING YOUR OWN SHORTHAND

You can also develop your own kind of shorthand; this will enable you to take down more material faster and with less effort. Many study guides teach specific formulas and codes for taking notes in shorthand. The problem with these methods is that you wind up having notes that are practically written in secret code. Don't make your notes overly complicated by developing all kinds of crazy signs and formulas. Find a way to take notes that make sense to you.

Here are some basic ways to develop a shorthand that is simple and easy to read. You can use any or all of these suggestions, depending on what makes the most sense to you.

AVOID COMPLETE SENTENCES

There's no reason why your notes have to be written in complete, grammatically correct sentences. Sentences are filled with words that aren't necessary for one to understand the gist of them. You can still understand the basic meaning of a sentence without using all the words in it. For example, you can leave out articles (the, a, an) and pronouns (he, she, they, it) and still understand the basic information.

EXAMPLE

The sentence:

You can omit the articles and pronouns from sentences and still be able to understand them.

can be rewritten as:

Omit articles pronouns from sentences still understand

Don't Worry About Spelling and Punctuation

If you try to spell everything correctly, you'll spend too much time worrying about it. Just write things the way they sound. You can check the spelling later. Sometimes using punctuation can help you write a quick definition, but it can also add unnecessary baggage to notes. You can read and understand most sentences perfectly well without it.

Keep Descriptions, Examples, and Anecdotes Brief

Very often, your professor will launch into a long description or anecdote as a means of illustrating or explaining some larger point. When the professor does this, you don't necessarily need to replicate the entire example or anecdote in your notes. You are better off listening, then using a few key words to sum up the example or anecdote. Those few words will usually be enough to trigger your memory of the entire account.

For example, a psychology professor might go into detail about various experiments and lab studies that either prove or disprove important points. You don't need to describe the whole study in your notes. You can simply write a few key words to help you remember who conducted the study, what was studied, and the result. For example, "James's Twins Study: Proved ESP doesn't work."

Abbreviate Only Repeated Key Terms

Using abbreviations is an excellent way to take notes more quickly. If you can reduce words to just a letter or two, it is obviously going to help you write faster. But be very careful. When you abbreviate too many terms, your notes become difficult to read. And if your notes don't make sense to you, then writing more quickly didn't really help you. You should therefore only abbreviate key terms that are repeated frequently throughout the lecture.

The best way to abbreviate is to use capital letters that stand for entire words. Usually you can just use the first letter of a word as its abbreviated form. It's a good idea to circle any abbreviations you use, so you'll recognize them.

The first time you come across an important term, write out the entire term and circle it. This will serve as a signal that you will be abbreviating this term from now on. Then, each time that term comes up, use the abbreviation and circle it.

For example, if you are attending a lecture on Freud, you can write

(Freud) the first time you hear his name

and abbreviate it as (F) each subsequent time.

To avoid confusion, you may sometimes want to use two or even three letters as an abbreviation. This can particularly help if the key term is itself made up of several terms.

For example, Gross National Product can be abbreviated (GNP).

The Trojan War might be abbreviated (TW).

Using two or three letters can also help avoid confusion between terms that start with the same letter.

For example, you can distinguish Dickens from Darwin within the same lecture as

(DK) and (DW).

In addition to using capital letters and initials, you can also abbreviate longer words by making them shorter. If a word or name has several syllables, you can use just the first syllable or two instead of writing out the entire word.

For example, the term autobiography can be abbreviated (autobio).

SIGNS AND SYMBOLS

It can also make note-taking much easier if you use signs and symbols for certain commonly repeated words. Again, the idea is to keep it simple. Don't fill up your notes with so many signs that they become impossible to read. Settle on a few common signs that you understand and use all the time. That way, when you read over your notes, you'll know what the signs mean right away without having to think about it.

Here are some suggestions for common symbols to help with your note-taking. You can use these or come up with your own.

$+$ in addition, and

$=$ equals, is the same thing, is defined as

$\neq$ is not the same thing, is different, unequal

i e	for example
≈	approximately
↗	increases
↘	decreases
⤳	has an affect or influence on
→	leads to, results in
@	at or about
✳ or !	this is an important point
VS.	compared to
− −	indicates a new point being raised
;	indicates a closely related point
( )	indicates additional information or a description of a point
⑦	I'm confused about this and need to double-check it

This last sign is very important as it signals where a problem is and that you need to get more information. Using this circled question mark, you can go on with your note-taking without worry. The important thing is not to get stuck on these confusing points—there'll be time to worry later, outside of class. Make certain to put the question mark in a circle so that you can distinguish it from other question marks.

CHARTS AND DIAGRAMS

A picture paints a thousand words and, when it comes to taking notes, drawing a picture is quicker and more concise than writing detailed explanations. You might, therefore, want to sketch charts and diagrams whenever possible. You don't need to be Picasso to draw a quick, easy-to-read sketch that conveys important information. Just don't overdo it; the purpose of including charts and diagrams is to save time and make your notes easier to understand.

If a particular term or concept lends itself to a simple diagram or chart, you should include it. Charts are particularly effective at indicating relationships among terms, people, and concepts. For example, if your professor is telling you about the British royal family, it is much easier to sketch a small family tree that indicates the family's relationships than to continue writing "and Henry married Eleanor and their children were Henry, Edward, and Mathilda, and they married . . ." Charts are also effective when a professor is comparing and contrasting various concepts. You can align the concepts side by side in your notebook to show how they differ.

Drawing a diagram is an effective way to provide a fast visual description of something that might take many sentences to describe. To describe the components of a neuron, for example, you'd have to write all this:

A neuron is made up of three key subdivisions: the dendrites, cell body, and axon. The cell body looks somewhat like an eye, with a nucleus at the center. The dendrites branch off from the cell body, sometimes quite extensively, like the branches of a tree without the leaves. The axon extends from the cell body, much like the trunk of a tree. Very often the end of the axon forks into several branches known as terminal endings.

Instead of writing all that, you can simply include this diagram:

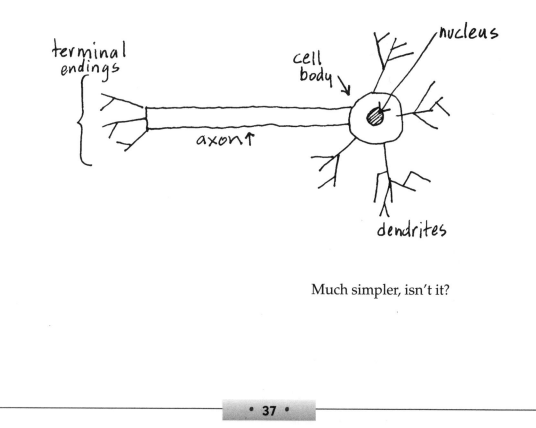

Much simpler, isn't it?

Sample Lecture Notes with Definitions

The next page shows how the notes from the previous exercise look when we include brief definitions and explanations with the key terms using the shorthand on page 36.

4. *Construct a Rough Outline*

The key terms we've been discussing don't exist in isolation; instead, they are part of a larger structure that is the professor's lecture. Each term ties in to some bigger topic or point being addressed. As you take them down, you can begin to construct a rough outline that will help you see how various terms are related and the topics they refer to.

Don't get stressed out at the idea of making an outline. You may be thinking that outlines are real headaches, that they are overly complicated and don't help all that much. The reason you feel that way is probably because you've been taught that there's only one way to make an outline and that it's a complex matter, with Roman numerals and letters. You don't have to worry about any of that. When we talk about making a rough outline for your notes, we are talking about a simple diagram that helps you to keep track of how various points and topics are related.

Before we do that, though, it will help if we look at how most lectures are structured.

Founder of Modern Psychoanalysis = Sigmund (Freud)

(F) worked in turn-of-century Vienna.

Model of Human Personality was one of (F's) big

theories; made up of id, ego, + superego

id = basic bio. urges (i.e. food and sex); relies on

pleasure principle

(ego) = tries to satisfy urges of id within real world;

relies on reality principle

superego = internal judge of bad and good;

conscience

(F) said conflict between id, (e,) and super- (e)

creates anxiety

id   superego

ego

repression = submerged forbidden urges, related to

anxiety

defense mechanisms (def mechs) created when

urges reappear

projection (example of def mech) = attribute urge to

others

denial (another def mech) = No way, José! not me.

* theory of dreams; in "The Interpretation of

Dreams" 1900

(F) said dreams depict wish fulfillment of repressed

urge i.e. "The Prisoner's Dream"

latent dream vs. manifest dream = actual urges vs.

disguised in images and symbols

WHAT'S IN A LECTURE?

In most cases, a lecture will focus on a *main topic*. At the start of the class, you should already have a general idea what this is. Professors who give out a syllabus or schedule of classes usually list the topic with a date. If you've gotten a schedule, make certain to see what your teacher has planned for each day. The day's required reading can also give you a sense of what the lecture topic will be.

Knowing the main topic is an important factor. As you take notes, remember that they all somehow fit in with this topic. Try to figure out what each new piece of information has to do with it. Some pieces may be central to the topic, while others may be less important. In your outline, indicate those that are more central to the main topic.

Within that main topic, there will be several additional topics your professor wants to address or points she wants to make. The important thing to keep in mind is that these almost always provide more detailed information about the main topic.

For example, if that day's lecture concerns a particular novel, the various topics might be the characters, plot, style, and author's background.

Example of a typical literature lecture:

MAIN TOPIC: A Novel

TOPIC: The Characters
SUBTOPIC: Specific Characters

TOPIC: The Plot
SUBTOPIC: Various Elements of the Plot
SUB-SUBTOPIC: The Climax

TOPIC: The Author
SUBTOPIC: Childhood and Teen Years
SUBTOPIC: Early Works
SUB-SUBTOPIC: Specific Works
SUB-SUBTOPIC: Critical Reaction

Similarly, the main topic for a history lecture might concern a major historical event, and the others might be factors that led up to that event.

As you can see, a number of subtopics may be addressed as well. These say something specific about each of the topics. Very often, subtopics will be examples that illustrate some major concept or principle. In a science or psychology class, for example, your professor might discuss different lab experiments that prove (or disprove) some theory.

MAKING A ROUGH OUTLINE IN YOUR NOTES

The key terms we've been talking about all somehow fit into this structure. Some might tie into topics, others into subtopics or sub-subtopics. Getting a sense of how these terms relate to one another is an important way of understanding them. It's a good idea, as you list these key terms, to indicate how they are related by constructing a rough outline. You can try to do this right in class during the lecture or when you work on your notes at home—whichever is easier for you.

For this outline, you need to group terms together so that you can see how they relate to one another and fall within specific topics and sub-topics. The best way to do this is by skipping lines between topics, and indenting terms beneath the blank lines to show that those terms are part of the topic.

Write a heading that describes each new topic in a few words, and underline it. Enter key terms as they come up by indenting them, about an inch in from the left-hand margin, beneath the topic heading. Doing so indicates the term is a part of the term above it. You can keep indenting as much as you like to indicate various subtopics and sub-subtopics. In general, the more you indent a term from the margin, the less important it is relative to the main topic.

Here is how a rough outline, without any Roman numerals or letters, might look for a typical lecture:

<u>MAIN TOPIC OF THE LECTURE</u>
(centered and underlined at top)

<u>TOPIC A (The first topic the teacher raises)</u>
   —Subtopic of Topic A (each new topic introduced with a dash)

   —Another Subtopic of Topic A

<u>TOPIC B (The next topic the teacher raises)</u>
   —Subtopic of Topic B
   —Another Subtopic of Topic B
   —Another Subtopic of Topic B
     —A Sub-Subtopic of B
     —Another Sub-Subtopic of B

REMEMBER, IT'S A *ROUGH* OUTLINE AND IT'S *YOUR* ROUGH OUTLINE

One reason students get nervous taking notes is because they think the professor has some specific outline in her own notes that they need to replicate exactly. It may be true that she does have such an outline, but you don't have to imitate it. The important thing is to take notes that make sense to you.

A good professor will make the organization of the lecture very clear, identifying new topics and important points, as well as the examples and subpoints. When the professor lectures, it's easy to take neatly organized notes in rough outline form. You just write down topics and terms in the order the professor introduces them.

However, not all professors are organized lecturers. Many will stray from whatever the topic is or whatever point they are making to discuss something else. This is known as a *digression*. When a professor digresses, just keep taking notes, but put them in parentheses to indicate they are digressive.

Some professors ramble on, without any clear organization to their points. They may fail to identify new topics, and jump back and forth randomly between points. In these cases, do the best you can. Keep taking notes and don't worry about keeping an outline. Try to see connections and relationships between various topics and key terms, and to indicate them in your notes. The thing to keep in mind is that this is just a rough sketch. Later, in stage two, you'll have plenty of opportunity to change your notes as much as you like.

Here's something else that should put your mind at ease: You don't necessarily have to have a rough outline at all! Your priority is still to get down the key terms. However, if making an outline is too much to worry about in one lecture, don't. The important thing is to get those key terms down. Later on, in stage two, you'll have more time to construct an outline.

Sample Rough Outline Notes

Here's how a rough outline for the psychology notes we've been taking would look:

SIGMUND FREUD'S THEORY OF PERSONALITY

Freud
—Founder of modern psychoanalysis
—Worked in turn-of-century Vienna
—Influential and controversial figure

Model of Human Personality = one of (F's) big theories
—Id = basic bio. urges (i.e., food and sex)
  —relies on pleasure principle; desire for instant gratification

—Ego = satisfies urges of id within real world
  —relies on reality principle

—Superego = internal judge of bad and good = conscience
— (Diagram: forces in conflict):

The id and superego try to influence the ego:

id   superego

                  ego

SIGMUND FREUD'S THEORY OF PERSONALITY (cont.)

Conflict and Anxiety

— (F) said conflict between id, (e,) and super-(e) creates anxiety

— Repression = submerging forbidden urges

— Defense mechanisms created when urges reappear

— Types of Def Mechs:

    — Projection = attribute urge to others

    — Denial = No way, José! Not me.

*(F's) Theory of Dreams

—The Interpretation of Dreams (1900)

— F. said dreams depict wish fulfillment of repressed urges

        (i.e., "The Prisoner's Dream")

— latent dream   vs.   manifest dream

  actual urges   urges disguised in
                  images, symbols

  not experienced   actually experi-
                   enced by dreamer

      GENERAL THEMES:

• Freud was a very influential but controversial figure

• Urges of the id are very powerful; can create anxiety

• Dreams are complex; more than meets the eye

5. Note general themes

As we have just noted, each lecture has a main topic and various subtopics. There might also be certain points, issues, and concepts that come up again and again within a single class and throughout the term. These are probably very important and should be noted.

It is also important that, at the end of each class, you take a few moments to jot down the major themes—the major topics and key points your professor made—from that day's lecture. Write these down as soon after the lecture has ended as possible, when the lecture is still fresh in your mind. Keeping track of these helps a great deal in preparation for exams. As a semester progresses, you'll begin to notice patterns in the lectures as certain themes recur. Very often, these themes are the major focus of examinations.

Ask yourself these questions: What were the major points the teacher made? What were the main topics? Try to pay particular attention to any opinions or stances about the material your professor might have conveyed to you. What seems to be the professor's personal opinion about the material? What does the professor seem to care the most about?

Sample Notes

The general themes of the lecture on Freud might be:

- Freud was a very influential but controversial figure
- Urges of the id are very powerful; can create anxiety
- Dreams are complex; more than meets the eye

There are a few tricks to figuring out what the most important points are within any given lecture.

NOTE WHAT'S REPEATED

Anything your professor says more than once is going to be important or it wouldn't be worth repeating. Make certain you put a star next to it and/or underline it, to signal that this is a very important point.

WATCH BODY LANGUAGE/LISTEN FOR TONE OF VOICE

People convey a great deal as they speak through their body language and tone of voice. Watch and listen more carefully to your professors to see what additional information you can discover.

You'll probably notice a change in the professor's expression and tone of voice when he addresses important information; he might sound more earnest, passionate, or serious. He might also speak more slowly and more clearly to emphasize a major point. In terms of body language, he might look directly at students in the class rather than at notes or facing the blackboard. In time, you can recognize specific actions. Many teachers take off their glasses, for example, to emphasize a key point. As you get to know your professor better, you'll become more adept at picking up these subtle clues.

FOCUS ON ENDINGS AND BEGINNINGS

The end of a lecture is the most important few minutes; this is when most professors will re-emphasize the main points. Sometimes, they will do this even as class is ending and students are rustling around with their books and belongings and walking out. Don't be one of those students who walk out of class the second time is up. For one thing, it's rude to the professor and makes a bad impression; but most importantly, you risk missing the most crucial information of the day. Make certain you write down the concluding remarks as carefully as you can.

Many professors also make key points at the start of the lecture, when they sum up points from the previous class and introduce the topic for that day. Make certain you arrive in class on time and pay special attention to what the professor says at the start. Throughout any lecture, listen for specific phrases and terms such as "to sum up," "in conclusion," "most especially," and "therefore," that indicate a professor is emphasizing a major point.

A WORD ON SEMINARS: TAKING NOTES ON DISCUSSIONS

Until now, we've primarily been addressing how to take notes during a lecture. These are classes where most of the time is spent listening to the professor speaking, imparting information. In addition to lectures, many of your classes might be seminars, where students participate in discussions with the professor. Discussions can sometimes happen before, after, or during a lecture, as well.

In taking notes during seminars or discussions, your concerns are somewhat different than in lectures. Discussions in seminars are less oriented toward key terms and much less structured. Here are some suggestions.

LISTEN MORE/WRITE LESS

Since the discussion will be open, you can feel free to sit back and listen more. By following the discussion carefully, you'll learn a great deal; but it won't necessarily be important for you to document everything that is said.

CONTINUE TO LOOK FOR KEY TERMS

Even in a discussion, key terms may come up. You can feel comfortable sitting back and listening, but watch out for them. Whenever the professor introduces new terms, make certain you write them down.

NOTE TOPICS OF DISCUSSION, BUT NOT SPECIFIC OPINIONS

Rather than write down everything that everyone says, note only the various topics that come up for discussion. What some other student thinks or feels about a given topic may help you understand the subject better, but you don't need to keep track of it in your notebook. No professor is going to test you on what another student thinks. However, having a record of the various topics that were covered in the seminar can give you a good sense of the kinds of things you'll be asked to discuss on an exam.

NOTE THE PROFESSOR'S OPINIONS

Your fellow students' opinions about material may not help on an exam, but your professor's views certainly might. After all, the professor is the one who makes the exams. Knowing how she thinks or feels about a topic can indicate what to emphasize in your preparation. When the professor speaks, listen to what she says and take notes. If the professor is expressing an opinion, just write, "Prof. thinks . . ."

STAGE TWO: NOTE-TAKING OUTSIDE OF CLASS

You might be thinking to yourself, aren't we done with note-taking already? Most students don't open their notebooks again until exam time, only to find they can't make sense out of much of what they've written. This produces a last-minute panic before the exam, as they struggle to relearn an entire semester's worth of material in a few days.

Instead of waiting until the last minute to figure out what you've got in your notes, you should get in the habit of working with them outside of the classroom.

1. Read Over Your Notes

Read your notes over at least once outside of class. This will serve two very important purposes: It will give you an opportunity to clarify anything that might be confusing, and it will help you learn the information. It also helps you develop a comfortable familiarity with the whole subject.

If you continue reading your notes, you'll become more and more immersed in your subject. When the exam comes, you'll feel like you have the information well at hand. Questions won't shock you because they seem alien; instead, they will elicit more educated responses.

Make reading over your notes a part of your study habits. You don't need to spend a great deal of time doing this— one or two hours a week per subject should be plenty of time. It's a good idea to do this on Friday or the weekend, so you can look at all your notes for the week. You don't have to read over your notes each night; in fact, you're better off leaving them alone for a few days. That way, you can approach them with a fresh eye.

2. Ask Yourself Questions

Don't read over your notes with a passive eye. You won't learn anything if you simply read without thinking about what you are reading. Instead, become as involved in your notes as you can. You can do this by considering these questions as you read:

- What does this mean? Does it make sense?
- How are these terms and topics related to one another?
- How do these terms and topics fit into the big picture?

3. Take Notes on Your Notes

If you have drawn a line down each sheet of notes, you should have a blank column to the left of the margin. You can now use this space to take notes on your notes. As you ask yourself the above questions, jot down answers here. If something confuses you, make a note of it.

You can also begin to make connections between various topics and terms in this space. During class, you might have tried to put your notes in a rough outline form. As you read over them, other relationships might become clear. No longer in the middle of a lecture, you now have a sense of the whole topic. You know where your professor is heading with the material. You have a better sense of what information is important and what doesn't matter as much. Jot down these thoughts in that left-hand margin. Remember also that you only took notes on one side of the page in class. You can use the back side now to jot down additional notes if you run out of room in the left-hand column.

4. Go to Other Sources

When you're finished reading over your notes, you should have marked areas or written down things that confuse you. Rather than letting those things go and praying they won't be on an exam, you should now take the time to figure them out.

Many people assume that the only source for information for class notes is the professor. That means you are entirely dependent on that one person for all the information. That's not fair to the professor and it's not fair to you. No one can communicate everything in a way that's entirely clear to every person. And as we've noted, some professors are much better at

communicating than others. At the same time, you've got to take some responsibility for your own education. You can't just sit back and rely on someone else to do all the work for you.

So, if something confuses you, try to educate yourself. There are several places where you can get help, and you can usually get it quickly and easily.

ADDITIONAL SOURCES OF INFORMATION

BORROW A FRIEND'S NOTES

No two people take exactly the same notes. There's a good chance that something you missed during a lecture was caught by someone else. If you missed some information or don't understand a section of your notes, look at a friend's notes. There's absolutely nothing wrong with sharing notes with a friend. Just make certain the friend is a reliable note-taker. You don't want to borrow notes from someone who doesn't take decent notes; you might wind up copying down incorrect information. However, if you know someone who seems to you like a smart student and efficient note-taker, you can begin to exchange notes on a regular basis.

CHECK YOUR TEXTBOOK

Your textbook for the course and any other required reading materials are valuable resources. Very often, the required reading assignments you do outside of class correspond to the lectures. These may cover many of the same topics and key terms discussed in the lecture. In a lecture, your comprehension is dependent on your listening skills, but in a textbook, where there is a written explanation laid out on the page, you have plenty of time to try to make sense of the material.

Check the index of the textbook for a listing of the topic or key term for which you want more information. The text's discussion of it may not necessarily be in the same chapter you read for homework. By checking the index, you'll be able to see all the pages in the book where the term is mentioned. For all you know, there is an excellent definition and description of a term in a chapter that's not assigned for homework.

FIND MORE SOURCES

Sometimes the textbook may still be rather confusing and not give the information you need. You might, therefore, want to turn to other sources. By reading someone else's explanation, you might begin to get a better understanding of the term. In general, the more explanations and interpretations you read, the more complete an understanding you gain.

Other textbooks are places to find more information. You don't have to buy another textbook, although you may want to if it will be very helpful. Many school libraries have several textbooks in the reference section. You also need not limit your research to textbooks. Go to the library and look for other books on the subject. If you need suggestions for books and articles to examine, check your textbook to see if there is a bibliography (list of sources used in the book) or a list of suggested further reading.

You can also check the subject catalog at the library for other books on that topic. You don't necessarily have to go in search of a specific source; you can simply to go the section of the library where that particular subject is shelved and browse. You'll be amazed at the kinds of things you find. Very often you will get lucky and find a book that covers the course topics clearly and concisely. There may even be a study guide with beautifully written summaries of all the topics you're researching. As you browse, check the tables of contents and indexes for the terms you need help with. You can also go to bookstores with decent academic and scholarly sources, such as campus bookstores, and browse.

The Internet is another valuable resource for getting information. If you have access to the Internet and are comfortable using it, you might find all kinds of materials that can help increase your understanding. Try to use a program that helps you find web sites by subject.

ASK THE PROFESSOR

Asking the professor for extra help—either by raising your hand in class or going to his office—might seem like the best way to get a quick and easy explanation of something that confuses you, but it isn't always. For one thing, there's no guarantee he will provide any better an explanation outside of class than he did inside of it. Another problem is that if you always rely on your professor for explanations, you give the impression that you cannot think for yourself. You don't want a professor to have that picture of you in mind when he assigns your grade.

If you are having real trouble understanding an important issue, feel free to go see the professor during office hours. In fact, going to see your professor a few times a semester is a good idea. That way the professor gets to know you by name and you give the impression of being a student who cares about the subject and your education. Just don't overdo it.

5. Fill in Additional Information

As you go about your additional research, make certain you take notes and fill in missing information in your notebook. If you found an explanation or definition that helps, write it in your notes. Use the space on the left side of the margin or the back of the sheet. You can also take notes on additional sheets and add them to the notes for that day's lecture in your loose-leaf notebook.

Sample Lecture Notes with Additional Notes and Information

The following page shows how the notes on Freud might look after you've worked with them outside of class:

SIGMUND FREUD'S THEORY OF PERSONALITY

Definition of psycho-analysis? In Bernstein text: Therapy based of F's theory of personali-ty; aims to help patient gain insight into his/her own subconscious.	Freud —Founder of modern psychoanalysis —Worked in turn-of-century Vienna —Influential and controversial figure

Why is F controversial? Cooper article says F, made generalizations based on a few personal, biased observations. Not scientifically valid. Cites several studies that disprove F's ideas.	<u>Model of Human Personality</u> = one of F's big theories
	—id = basic bio. urges (i.e., food and sex)
	  —relies on pleasure principle; desire for instant gratification
	—ego = satisfies urges of id within real world
	  —relies on reality principle
	—superego = internal judge of bad and good = conscience
	
	— (Diagram: Forces in Conflict):
	The id and superego try to influence the ego:

id   superego

ego

SIGMUND FREUD'S THEORY OF PERSONALITY

How does (F.) say suppression happens? *Textbook discusses key role of parents who <u>punish and disapprove.</u> Other def. mechs?*	<u>Conflict and Anxiety</u>
	— F said conflict between id, (e), and super-(e) creates anxiety
	— Repression = submerging forbidden urges
	— Defense mechanisms created when urges reappear
	— Types of (Def Mechs:)
	   — projection = attribute urge to others
	   — denial = No way, José! Not me.

Other def mechs? *-reaction formation* *-displaced aggression* *-sublimation* *(all these are defined in the book)*	
How do dreams play into other psychologists' theories? I seem to remember Jung was into dreams. Remember to compare notes on Freud with notes on Jung!	<u>* F's Theory of Dreams</u> —<u>The Interpretation of Dreams</u>, 1900 —F. said dreams depict wish fulfillment of repressed urges (i.e. "The Prisoner's Dream") —<u>latent dream</u> vs. <u>manifest dream</u> (actual urges (urges disguised in not experienced) images, symbols actually experienced by dreamer

GENERAL THEMES:
- Freud was a very influential but controversial figure
- Urges of the id are very powerful; can create anxiety
- Dreams are complex; more than meets the eye

6. Rewrite Your Notes (Optional)

Some people believe in rewriting all their notes. They go home each night and do it meticulously in another notebook. That's pretty much a waste of time and paper. Rewriting doesn't help at all if you haven't really read and thought about the notes, and worked to try to understand them.

However, with the method we've been discussing, you have worked on your notes outside of class. In the process, they may have become disorganized and messy, especially as you've added information from other sources. In this case, you may want to rewrite them. You may, for example, want to incorporate the information from the left side of the margin into the notes on the right side. If you have the time, by all means go ahead and do it.

Something else might have happened in this process of re-examining and researching your notes. You may have developed a much better understanding of how various topics and terms are related. You may see that certain points go together in a certain way, while others belong somewhere else or are not very important. If this has happened, you may want to rewrite your notes with a new rough outline that makes more sense to you. This may include information in a very different way than you professor delivered it in class. But that's fine. The important thing is that these notes now make sense to you.

Sample of Rewritten, Reorganized Notes

Here's how the notes on Freud might look after you've worked on their organization and rewritten them:

SIGMUND FREUD'S THEORY OF PERSONALITY

Freud =

—Founder of modern psychoanalysis, which Bernstein defines as therapy based on (F's) theory of personality that aims to help the patient gain insight into his/her own subconscious.

    —Influential and controversial figure—Cooper article says F made generalizations based on a few personal, biased observations; not scientifically valid.

Model of Human Personality = Major theory of (F)

—id=basic bio. urges (i.e., food and sex); relies on pleasure principle

—ego=satisfies urges of id within real world; reality principle

—superego=internal judge of bad and good; the conscience

(*NOTE: Prof. said id + superego try to influence behavior of the ego.)

Conflict and Anxiety

According to F:

anxiety= conflict between id, e, and super-e

repression= submerging forbidden urges

defense mechanism created when urges reappear (Textbook says suppression results when parents punish/disapprove).

Types of def. mechs:

projection, denial, reaction formation, displaced aggression, sublimation

SIGMUND FREUD'S THEORY OF PERSONALITY (cont.)

<u>F's Theory of Dreams (Fr. Interpretation of Dreams, 1900)</u>
—depict <u>wish fulfillment</u> of repressed urges
—latent dream   vs.   manifest dream
actual urges not experienced   urges disguised in
     symbols, images
         actually experienced by dreamer

(*NOTE: compare to notes on Jung and theory of collective
    unconscious.)

GENERAL THEMES:
* Freud was a very influential but controversial figure.
* Urges of the id are very powerful; can create anxiety.
* Dreams are complex; more than meets the eye.

Is it cake yet?

If you've followed the method we've just outlined, both inside and outside of the classroom, you will have accomplished a great deal. Not only will you have notes that accurately represent the lecture, you'll also have begun to process the material, making it part of your general knowledge. As we'll see, this will make preparing for exams much less stressful for you than for most of your classmates.

The important thing to remember about notes, at least as we've been approaching them, is that they are never really finished products. Most students think their notes are done when the lecture is over. This thinking creates problems that come back to haunt them at exam time. These students open their notebooks and find they can't make heads or tails out of much of what they wrote. Moreover, they have to struggle to memorize these notes that they are seeing as if for the first time.

Instead of thinking of notes as finished, the method we've outlined looks at them as a continuing process. Your notes are not finished the second class ends; instead, you add, expand, and change them to reflect new information you discover. Nothing says you can't go back to reread and add to your notes. While this should be done each week for that week's notes, you can keep going back to these notes throughout the semester. As you learn new information, in lectures and reading, you may think back on previous information. You may make connections between different points from different lectures. You may also gain a greater understanding of earlier information.

This reflects a more accurate view of how learning takes place. You don't learn by ingesting entire blocks of information in one gulp. The mind processes information over time. As you hear and read and discover new information, your mind connects it with previous information. Something that you didn't understand before may suddenly click into place. As you gain more understanding of something, you make it a part of your overall knowledge. That means it stays with you for long periods of time—right through an exam and beyond.

Important Points to Remember

1. Effective notetaking starts with effective listening.

2. You don't have to write down everything the teacher says; in fact, you shouldn't even try to.

3. Notes aren't finished when you leave the classroom; you should continue working with them and thinking about them. This will help you learn the material and save time studying for exams later on.

4. You don't need to rely on what the teacher says as your only source of information; feel free to consult other sources for additional information or to clarify points that confuse you.

5. Develop your own shorthand for taking notes quickly. Just make certain your notes make sense to you.

6. Maintain a sense of the overall topic of each lecture and note general themes.

CHAPTER 3

Reading Texts

WRONG WAYS TO READ

Highlighter Helen

Helen buys highlighters by the truckload. When she sets about her required reading assignment for class, she sits with her hot pink highlighter in hand, brandishing it like a machete. As she reads, she highlights anything that looks important, anything that is worth remembering, anything she might be tested on, and anything that confuses her. When her mind starts to wander, she doesn't really worry; as long as something is highlighted, she thinks she has "covered" it. When she's done reading, more of the page is hot pink than white. Helen is satisfied with her work, certain that she's read the chapter thoroughly. So she is quite surprised when she does poorly on the final exam. And that's not the worst of it. When she tries to sell back her $50 textbook at the end of the semester, the book store won't take it. As the clerk tells her, "Who wants to buy a hot pink textbook?"

Bored Beth

Beth sits down to read an article entitled, "Semiology and Structuralist Criticism." "Yuck," she thinks, "this sounds totally boring." She reads the first few sentences and comes across terms she's never seen before, like "signifier" and "syntax," and begins to roll her eyes. "This is soooo boring," she whines to herself. She reads another line, then glances out the window. She stares at the sky, the trees, and a cute dog catching a Frisbee on the grass, then goes back to the article. She's forgotten what she's read, so she has to start reading the article from the beginning. Rubbing her aching head, she reads the first two paragraphs, and soon finds herself thinking about her weekend plans. What will she do Saturday night? Who will she go out with? She forces herself to go back to her reading, but once again has lost her place. She starts the first sentence again, then decides the reading is just too boring and probably won't be on the test anyway. Unfortunately, she's wrong.

Super Speed-Reading Stan

Looking over the syllabi for his courses for the fall, Stan realizes that to do all the required reading for his five courses will take about forty hours a week. He also realizes that to do all that reading is practically impossible if he is also going to attend classes, eat, and sleep. On the side of a bus he sees what he thinks is his salvation, an advertisement for a course in Super Speed-Reading. He proceeds to pay $500 for a three-hour seminar on super speed-reading, given at a local motor lodge. In the course, he learns to run his fingers down the page as fast as he can, reading just the middle section of each line. The instructor assures the class that although they may feel they are missing a great deal, the brain still manages to process everything it sees, even at this speed. A proud graduate of the course, Stan sits down to read the "Semiology" article at a super-speed. He finishes the article in four and a half minutes—and doesn't understand a word of it.

READING ISN'T ALWAYS AS EASY AS A-B-C

When you aren't in your classes taking notes, you are probably going to be spending long hours hitting the books. Reading textbooks and other required sources is a major part of the educational process. Yet many students go about their reading in completely the wrong way, much like the three readers just discussed. We all think we can read fairly well; after all, most of us have been doing it since elementary school. But reading serious academic texts is much more difficult than the other kinds of reading we are accustomed to. It requires a whole new set of skills and techniques.

WHAT'S SO TOUGH ABOUT READING?

There are several reasons why the reading you have to do for school is going to be difficult.

1. Reading Overload

When you add up the amount of required reading for each week, you'll probably find it will take hours and hours to complete all your reading assignments, more than seems humanly possible. You could try to read everything assigned, but you'll wind up spending most of your week doing it. You won't have much time to relax or socialize. You also probably won't be reading very efficiently; you won't really understand everything you read, and the reading ultimately won't help you on exams.

The fact, is you don't have to read everything you are assigned. Professors generally assign far more reading than is

absolutely necessary; they'll assign entire chapters or articles when only certain sections will be relevant. And you don't need to take a super speed-reading course. The most effective strategy is to be a selective reader who can assess what material is important and worth reading, and what isn't.

2. Poorly Written Texts

If you're having trouble understanding a certain source, particularly a textbook, you may be tempted to think it's your fault. You probably believe that a source as authoritative as a textbook has to be good, especially if it was assigned by a professor. There are indeed many very well-written textbooks that are truly informative and clearly organized. But there are also many poorly written textbooks, sloppily thrown together, that give students more headaches than helpful information. Don't assume that everything your teacher gives you is going to be expertly written, not to mention factually correct. Very often, teachers assign readings from textbooks as a kind of backup, to make certain that if a topic or issue isn't adequately covered in class, the students will have a chance to make up for it in their reading. The professor may not have even read the assignment herself! You're the one

who is going to have to try to make sense of it. In this chapter, you'll learn tips on how to make sense of your textbook—and how to be a critic of required sources, evaluating just how reliable and helpful they really are. As we'll see, if a source is poorly written, you can toss it and still do well in class.

3. Difficult Texts

As you advance in your education, you'll find that the kind of reading you are required to do is much more complex than you've encountered before. It's partly because you'll be coming up against more sophisticated vocabulary and terms, but it will also be due to the style in which academic materials are written. Academic sources are written in a way that is distinct from writing in a magazine or best-selling novel. People in academia are accustomed to this style, but it's going to be new for you. Like learning a new language, it will take time to pick up "academese" and feel comfortable reading it. You'll have to struggle with some of the texts you encounter, working very hard just to make sense of them. That's not necessarily a bad thing; struggling with a difficult text can be exciting and helps make the reading process more interesting. Best of all, the feeling that you've finally "got it" is extremely gratifying.

The main problem with these kinds of difficult texts is not the way they're written; it's the "boredom" they nevertheless can generate. When students encounter a difficult text, many are quick to dismiss it rather than take the time to work with the text and get to understand it. Don't fall into the "boring" trap. When you sit down with a difficult text, be prepared to fight a bit—and reap the rewards when you're finished.

4. The Wandering Mind

The most common problem students face when reading for classes isn't tough vocabulary or work overload; it's the way their minds seem to wander, finding interest in everything other than the assignment. There are all kinds of distractions to keep your eye and your mind from the page; don't underestimate how powerful they can be! Many distractions come from the surroundings—noises, music, other people in the room, the telephone. Just as many, though, come from within your head. You'll be reading along and suddenly your thoughts will turn to something completely different—a conversation you had earlier in the day, your plans for later in the day, your shopping list,

your favorite episode of *The Brady Bunch.*

Just about anything can pop into your head when you should be focusing on reading. And once you are distracted, it's all the more difficult to get back on track. You might have to start from the beginning of the chapter, which makes the total time spent reading much longer than it needs to be. Or, you might just keep reading without even realizing how much you've missed while you were thinking about other things.

Don't feel bad if your mind tends to wander—you're not alone, and it's understandable. It's not easy to concentrate on required readings, especially if the topic doesn't interest you or the books themselves are poorly written. But there is hope.

Did you ever read a book that you just couldn't put down? A murder mystery? A trashy romance? Chances are you have, and you became so involved in the plot that your mind never once wandered. Why should it be different reading textbooks and other required assignments? The difference is that when you pick up a real page-turner, you have a vested interest in what you are reading that keeps you engaged. Very simply, you want to find out what will happen. Who is the killer? Will he murder the heroine? Will the main couple wind up together, or lose one another forever? That interest keeps you so deeply involved that you don't want to turn away, even for a second.

In this chapter, we'll learn a way to read that helps spark the same kind of involvement with your textbook as you experience with a page turner. Of course, you're not likely to find a textbook you just can't put down; but you can learn ways to become much more interested in and engaged with whatever you read. Honest.

Summer Reading:

A List of Accessible, Readable Books That Will Teach You a Whole Lot About Something

Ways of Seeing by John Berger
The Power of Myth by Joseph Campbell and Bill Moyers
The Narrative of Frederick Douglass
The Autobiography of Benjamin Franklin
Civilization and Its Discontents by Sigmund Freud
The Madwoman in the Attic by Sandra Gilbert and Susan Gubar
The Transitive Vampire: A Handbook of Grammar for the Innocent, the Eager and the Doomed by Karen E. Gordon
A Brief History of Time: From the Big Bang to Black Holes by Stephen Hawking
The Tao of Pooh and *The Te of Piglet* by Benjamin Hoff
The Woman Warrior by Maxine Hong Kingston
The Painted Bird by Jerzy Kosinski
The Structure of Scientific Revolutions by Thomas Kuhn
The Armies of the Night by Norman Mailer
The Celluloid Closet by Vito Russo
Cosmos by Carl Sagan
You Just Don't Understand: Women and Men in Conversation by Deborah Tannen
Riding the Iron Rooster by Paul Theroux
The Aeneid by Virgil (translated by Robert Fitzgerald)
A Room of One's Own by Virginia Woolf

Becoming an Active Reader

In the last chapter, we saw that one of the reasons taking notes during lectures is difficult is because people tend to be passive listeners. Well, being a passive reader is just as much of a problem.

We think that when we sit down, open a book, and read, we somehow will absorb it all. In actuality, you can read every word on the page and not understand a bit of it. In order to become an *effective* reader, you have to be an *active* reader. That means doing more than just looking at the words on the page; it means becoming involved with the material and *thinking* while you read.

In this chapter, we're going to learn a strategy for effective reading of academic materials. You'll notice that it is very similar to the process for taking notes outlined in the last chapter. That's because in both cases the goal is the same: to become a more active listener/reader who truly absorbs and understands the information being conveyed.

These are the basic steps of the strategy:

1. Know where you're headed—and why
2. Make a rough outline
3. Watch for key terms/take notes with brief definitions
4. Note general themes
5. Write a response

In the detailed description of the steps that follow, we'll primarily be discussing ways to read a textbook. Most courses you take will have a textbook that has been written for that subject, especially in the survey and introductory courses you take in high school or as a college freshman and sophomore. This strategy can also be adapted for other kinds of sources, which we'll describe at the end of the chapter.

Throw Out the Highlighters!

The strategy for reading you are about to learn is not only going to help you read more effectively; it's going to save you money! Many students think that as long as they highlight sections of a chapter, they've read it. In reality, highlighting a passage only means that they've looked at it. They haven't necessarily thought about it and absorbed what they've read. When it comes time to study for exams, they then have to go back and reread all those highlighted sections. That takes a whole lot of time that could be spent studying.

There is a more serious problem, though, with highlighting. Like most students, you'll probably

want to sell back some (or all) of your textbooks at the end of the semester. Textbooks today are very expensive, often costing between thirty and fifty dollars. When bookstores buy back used books, they always offer more money for books that are unmarked. The more marked up or highlighted a book is, the less money they'll offer. If a book is seriously marked up, they might not even buy it back! But if you don't highlight or mark up your book, you can sell it back for a decent amount of money.

You'll be glad to know that our reading strategy doesn't require that you write in or mark up the textbook at all. Believe it or not, you'll read much more efficiently and be better prepared for exams than if you did highlight. If you do want to write in the textbook, though, do it in pencil. That way, you can erase it at the end of the semester and get more money for your books.

Textbook Bargains—Saving Money on Your Books

Buying textbooks and other reading materials for classes can be a costly venture. There are, however, a number of ways to save some money.

Buy used textbooks. Your school bookstore will usually sell several used copies of books required for your course, especially if they are popular books used in different classes. The problem with buying used textbooks is that they are often marked up by previous students. Try to get to the bookstore early in the semester so you can rummage through the pile of books and choose one that is relatively clean. Should you purchase a book that has notes or highlighted sections, try to ignore them as you read. Just because some other student felt the sections were relevant doesn't mean they will be to you.

Check used bookstores. If your school bookstore doesn't have any used copies of books you need, try checking local bookstores that specialize in used books. These shops occasionally carry used textbooks, but you are more likely to find other sources, such as novels, plays, and biographies. Either way, it's worth seeing what they have available. Again, go early in the semester, as other students might have the same idea.

Borrowing books from friends. Many people take the same or similar courses. Ask around to see if anyone owns the books you need, and then try to borrow or even purchase the books from them. There is a chance, though, that your friend has an older edition of the book; just be aware of this as you read it. If possible, consult a current edition and note any changes. You can skim the current edition in a bookstore, or ask someone in your class if you can borrow theirs.

Sharing Books. Some students who are friends and enrolled in the same class consider chipping in for the books and sharing them. This does save money but is not recommended, since sharing can cause more problems than it's worth. Because you both need access to the books, each person has less less time available to read and study them. This is particularly a problem before major exams, when you both will want to consult the book for an extended period of time. However, if you are really trying to save money, this is an option—you'll just need to organize a tight schedule that will allow you enough access to the books.

(cont.)

Textbook Bargains—Saving Money on Your Books *(cont.)*

The Library. The school library will probably carry many of the sources that your teacher requires for your class. If you can use a library book, you will obviously save a great deal of money. However, there are certain drawbacks to depending on library books. You may need a certain book throughout the semester, but you will only be able to take it out of the library for a few weeks. Moreover, other students—even those who are not in your class—will also want those books; and because the library will have a limited number of copies, there's no guarantee you'll get the books when you need them. If a required book for your class is going to be used repeatedly, then you should probably not rely on using a library copy. However, if it is a book that will only be used for a week or two (such as a novel you are reading for an English class), then you might consider trying to get the book out from the library.

If the book is located in the reference section of the library, as many textbooks are, you don't have to worry about finding it because they can't be taken out. You just need to be willing to sit with the book in the library and take notes. Many professors also put the books required for their courses on reserve in the library, which means the books cannot leave the library and students are given a limited amount of time to read them. If books are on reserve, you know you'll be able to get hold of them at some point; if they are not, try suggesting that to the professor that she place them there for everyone.

Selling back books. At most school bookstores, you can sell your books back at the end of the semester and receive a partial refund. Keep in mind, however, that the cleaner your copy is, the more money you will get back. If the book is heavily marked up, the bookstore may refuse to buy it back at all. If you are planning to sell your books, avoid using highlighters or taking notes in the book. That shouldn't be a problem; if you follow the note-taking strategy outlined in this book, you won't need to highlight or write in the book. If for some reason you do want to write in the book, do it lightly and in pencil so it can be erased.

WHERE TO READ

Many study guides insist that the only way you can read is holed up at some library cubicle, sitting on a hard-backed chair. While that will certainly minimize outside distractions, it won't necessarily make you a better reader. You are going to spend many hours reading each semester, so you may as well read somewhere that you feel comfortable. Of course, you don't want to be so comfortable that you fall asleep. But if you are serious about your work and actually complete assignments, there's no reason you can't read in your room or even in bed.

No matter where you read, you do need to minimize outside distractions. For example, you don't want to read in your room if roommates or friends keep interrupting you. By the same token, studying in the library won't help you if friends keep coming over asking how you are doing and what you thought of last night's football rally. Find an isolated spot in the library where there won't be many people walking by.

No matter where you decide to study, make certain it is well lit. You're going to be reading a great deal while you are in school, and it does take a toll on the eyes. If a room isn't well lit, you'll find yourself straining to see and getting headaches. Some areas of the library may be dimmer than your own desk at home.

It's okay to listen to music while you read, at home or in the library (as long as it's on a portable headset). Listening to music drowns out many of the outside noises that can distract you. However, you should be careful about the kind of music you choose. You want to have music on that will be in the background, rather than attract your attention. Something old, which you are familiar with and makes you feel relaxed, will probably be better than something you just bought. Keep the music on lower than you would normally listen to it.

In Chapter 5, we'll be talking much more about finding the best places to study. The important thing to remember here is that there is no right or wrong place to read as long as you feel comfortable *and* make progress. In any setting, do what you need to do in order to minimize outside distractions.

GETTING STARTED

The reading strategy outlined in this chapter involves taking notes while you read. You might, therefore, want to read at a desk or table; if not, bring some kind of flat surface (a large hardcover book or lap caddie) on which to write.

You'll also need the same loose-leaf paper you use for taking notes in class. Make certain to write the date and author or title of the material you are reading at the top of each page. That way, if the sheets get out of order, you can easily put them back.

WHAT TO DO WITH THE NOTES WHEN YOU'RE DONE

After each reading assignment, when you're done taking notes, you should put them in the same notebook binder you keep your classroom notes in.

If the reading assignments don't coordinate with the lectures, you might keep the reading notes in a separate section of your binder. But usually, your professor will coordinate reading assignments with lectures. If

this is the case, then keep the reading notes alongside the lecture notes. By keeping lecture and reading notes side by side, you'll be able to observe the ways in which the reading assignments and lectures fit together. For example, you'll see if certain points are covered repeatedly—an indication they are especially important and likely to show up on an exam.

If your professor has assigned a reading for a particular day, you might want to bring your notes from your reading with you to the lecture; this will enable you to refer to them. For example, if the professor introduces a new term you recognize from your reading, you can quickly check for the proper spelling. Additionally, you might be able to save time. For example, if you know you've already defined a particular term in your reading notes, you won't have to repeat it.

Make certain you only bring notes to class that correspond to that day's reading assignment. Leave the rest at home in your binder so that you don't risk losing them.

Effective Reading: A Step-By-Step Strategy

Much of the reading you will be required to do in school will be in textbooks, books that are specifically written to be used for educational purposes. In many courses, you will also be required to read other materials, such as various kinds of books and articles. Although the following section specifically refers to reading a chapter of a textbook, the basic step-by-step strategy outlined here can be applied to just about anything you read for school. Later in the chapter, we'll discuss the special considerations of different types of required reading materials.

1. Know Where You're Headed—and Why

When you go on a trip, you usually have a destination in mind and a route planned before you go. You know exactly where you are going and why—and that's what keeps you from getting lost. The same holds true for reading. If you don't want your mind to wander, make certain you know right from the beginning where you're

headed and the route you are taking.

Before you begin reading, think a bit about *what* you are reading. What is the title of the chapter, article, or text? Does it give you any hint as to what you can expect? As with classroom lectures, each chapter or article you read will have a main topic. Make certain you know the topic before you start to read.

Next, try to get a sense of the chapter's contents. Glance through the chapter and look at the various headings and subheadings of different sections. Look at the pictures, diagrams, and charts. Try to get a sense of what topics are included within a chapter, how they relate to one another, and how they come together within the main topic.

Keeping the "big picture" in mind as you read will help keep you on track. You'll have a sense of how each section fits into the overall text, and you'll know how much more material you have ahead of you, which can help you plan your time. Also, a sense of the chapter's contents can help you read more selectively.

Try to keep in mind not only what you are reading, but why. Of course, one reason is because the material is required reading. But if that is the only reason, you are going to get bored pretty quickly. Each chapter should somehow contribute to your understanding of the course material, as well as to your general knowledge. If you can designate a purpose for each thing you read, you'll feel better about doing the work. You won't be reading just to please the professor, but because you see some value in fulfilling the assignment.

Think about some of these questions:

- What do you think your professor is hoping you will gain by reading this?
- What might you personally gain from reading this?
- How does the chapter or text fit in with the overall subject matter of the course?

- How does the text fit in with the current course topics (i.e., the lectures for that week)?
- Does the chapter build on previous material? How?
- Does the chapter prepare you for upcoming topics? How?
- Is anything in the chapter familiar to you? What? Where and when did you first learn it? What did you already learn? What in the chapter is new to you?

Thinking about these questions will help you become actively involved in the reading assignment right from the start. Contemplating these issues helps you evaluate how important the assignment is to you, which will also help you be a selective reader. These questions also help you gain a more personal interest in the reading by connecting it with your overall knowledge. That way, you won't feel you are reading just because it's required, but because it can somehow enhance your understanding of the subject matter.

2. Make a Rough Outline

Just as you do when taking notes during a lecture, you should make a rough outline of all reading assignments. This will fulfill two important purposes. First, taking notes will give you something to *do* while you read, making you more of an *active* reader with a purpose. This, in turn, will keep you focused on the assignment and minimize the tendency to let your mind wander. Second, these outlines will help you remember the material. When it comes time to study for an exam, you can read over these notes rather than have to go over large, highlighted chunks of text.

To make the rough outline, you merely need to note various topics and subtopics. You'll find that making an outline will be easier than taking notes during a lecture. Most textbooks, unlike most professors, make it very clear how they are organized. Many books list, either in the table of contents or at the start of the chapter beneath the title, the topics covered in a particular chapter. Within a chapter, the topics, subtopics, and sub-subtopics usually have clearly labeled headings and subheadings. Most books differentiate between the more important topics and the lesser ones by changing the typeface style of the headings. For example, the more important headings will be larger and/or in boldface, while less important ones will be smaller and in lighter or italic type.

As you read, watch for headings and subheadings and, as they come up, write them down. As with any outline, the less important a topic is, the more you indent it on your paper.

3. *Watch for Key Terms; Take Notes with Brief Definitions*

In the last chapter, we saw that most lectures center on key terms. Most textbook chapters also center on key terms—names, dates, facts, theories, and concepts—that are new to you. And just as you take notes in lectures, you should look for the key terms and include them in your reading notes. It will probably be easier to identify these terms in textbooks than during lectures because in most textbooks they are in boldface or italics. Try to fit them into your rough outline by placing them beneath the same heading or subheading in your notes as they appear in the chapter.

You should also try to include brief definitions of the key terms. You don't need to write these definitions in complete sentences. Use the same shorthand you would for taking lecture notes. As with your lecture notes, you don't need to write in complete sentences or worry about grammar and punctuation. Feel free to use abbreviations and symbols. Just remember, though, that the notes should still be easy for you to read.

Don't copy down the exact, word-for-word explanation of the term as you find it in the text. Instead, use your own words to define the term as briefly as possible. If, as you read over your notes later on, you don't understand something, you can always refer back to the textbook.

4. Note General Themes

When you are finished with a chapter, you should take a few minutes to jot down its general themes. To help you identify these, you might consider these questions:

- What seemed to be the author's main concerns in this chapter?
- What ideas, topics, or points were mentioned more than once?
- Was there any kind of introduction or conclusion? If so, what points did the author make here?
- Did you get a sense of the author's opinion or stance on the material he or she was addressing? What was it?

These notes will be instrumental in helping you prepare for exams. In addition to helping you recall the overall content of a reading assignment, they will enable you to compare the key themes of all the reading assignments and classroom lectures. This will help you gain a sense of how various parts of the course fit together. And it's a safe bet that when themes show up throughout the semester, they're likely to appear on an exam.

5. Write a Response

In the last chapter, we saw that effective note-taking doesn't end when you leave the classroom. By the same token, the reading process doesn't have to end when you get to the last word of the chapter.

When they get to the last sentence of a reading assignment, most students think, "Whew! That's finished. What a relief!" and close the book without giving it another thought. They don't realize that a great deal of the work they've just done will have been a waste of time. While they have read the assignment, they have not really *thought* about it. They have looked at the words on the page, but they haven't thought about what they mean. They don't know if they even understood what they have just read. In short, they haven't really learned anything based on what they've read.

If you want to learn something from what you read, it is crucial that

you *think* about it after you've finished reading. An excellent way to keep you thinking is to write a reading response.

To write a reading response, you simply write whatever you want about what you've read.

First, close the book and put it aside, and take out a few sheets of fresh paper. Draw a line down the page so that you have a left-hand margin of about three inches. Write your response only on the right side of the margin; you'll use the space on the left-hand side later on.

A reading response is *not* a summary of the chapter. Instead, it's your opportunity to engage with the material you've just read. Think of yourself as having a conversation with the author of the text. This is your chance to share whatever is on your mind.

Here are some questions you might address in your response:

- What is your emotional reaction to what you've read? Do you like what you read? Why or why not? How did reading the text make you feel? How do you think the writer wants you to feel?
- What points do you think are most important to the writer? Did the writer successfully convey these to you?
- What parts, if any, did you have trouble understanding? Why? What made it confusing?
- What questions about the text do you still have? Make certain you list questions about any terms, topics, or points you didn't understand. You can also list questions you have that arise from the reading. Are there additional questions about the subject matter that were not addressed in the text? By the way, these questions

don't necessarily have to be answered right away. They may be answered as you read more throughout the semester; or, they may never be answered.

- How does this text connect with other things you've learned? Does it tie into things you've studied in other courses? Does the reading remind you of anything else?

These are just suggestions of topics you can address in your response. When you sit down to do the reading response, let yourself write whatever comes into your head. Set a time limit during which you will write about the assignment without stopping. You can set a limit of five or ten minutes per assignment. Or you might set a page limit of one or two pages of response for every five you read. It's up to you how you do this; just make certain you always write some kind of response.

Even though you write the responses *after* you finish reading, writing them is going to help you become a more effective reader; they will encourage you to be a more active participant in the reading process. Many students approach required readings like mindless robots; they focus on the words on the page and try to suppress any of their own thoughts or feelings. But the mind wants to be more involved than that. And if it's not involved, it is going to wander.

You are not a robot. You are a real person who has thoughts, feelings, and opinions about what you read. You are allowed to like something you read, or to hate it. You are allowed to be confused or excited. Your response gives you the opportunity to express all the things you are thinking and feeling.

Once a week, set aside time to read over your responses to all the reading assignments for the previous week. Pay special attention to any questions you had about things that you did not understand, and make a note of them in the space on the left-hand side of the margin. You can then go to other sources for more detailed explanations of these tricky concepts. You can consult other textbooks or books on the same subject. You can also ask friends in the class or the professor about difficult points you don't understand. Use the left-hand column to take notes from these other sources.

You may want to read your responses throughout the semester, especially as you get closer to an exam. You'll find that as a course progresses and you get deeper into the subject matter, you'll gain a better understanding of key concepts. You'll also start to see how different concepts are related to one another, and how they fit into the "big picture" of the course. A reading assignment that initially confused you may make sense later in the semester. Long after you've completed a reading, you might begin to see how the material relates to another reading or topic covered in class. You can then go back over your initial response and make additional notes that indicate what you now understand.

Sample Textbook Chapter and Notes

Here is a sample passage from a textbook, along with the notes and response a student might write after completing the reading. If you like, you can treat this like an exercise. Read the following textbook entry, take your own notes, and write your own response. Then compare it to the notes and response that follow the excerpt.

CHAPTER 2

Classical Theater
• • • • • • • • • • • • • • • • •

In this chapter we cover:
- Ritual Origins of Theater
- Customs and Trends of Greek Theater
- The Development of Greek Tragedy
- Architecture of the Theater

The Origin of Tragedy

Although exact accounts of the origins of theater in ancient Greece do not survive, many believe it evolved out of religious rituals. These rituals were primarily in honor of Dionysus, the Greek god of wine and fertility.

According to Aristotle's *Poetics*, the earliest account of the origins of Greek drama still in existence, tragedy grew out of *dithyrambs*, hymns sung and danced to honor Dionysus. Over time, dithyrambs became quite elaborate, involving entire choruses who sang and danced. Occasionally the chorus related stories and episodes derived from myth.

Although the exact manner in which the dithyramb developed into tragedy remains unclear, people speculate it was the result of an innovation made on the part of a member of the chorus who stepped out of the chorus and added additional lines, spoken as a character. Although there is no solid evidence to support this, the person credited with this innovation is *Thespis*, who, as a playwright himself, would go on to win the first dramatic contest presented in Athens.

Dramatic Festivals

The Greeks paid homage to their gods at elaborate annual festivals. The primary ones were held in honor of Dionysus, including the City Dionysia, held in Athens. As far as we know, this was the first festival at which drama was presented and tragedy officially sanctioned. Playwrights presented several plays throughout the festival, and the winner was granted a prize.

Development of Tragedy

Tragedy is usually dated back to 534 B.C. when it was given official recognition as a part of the festival called the City Dionysia. Unfortunately, no drama from the sixth century survives. What we know about Greek tragedy comes from the work that remains from the fifth century. All tragedies that survive from the fifth century are the works of three playwrights: Aeschylus, Sophocles, and Euripedes.

The oldest surviving plays are by Aeschylus, who is credited with the innovation of adding a second actor to the stage. Prior to Aeschylus, custom dictated that only one actor appear on stage, in addition to the members of the chorus and the choral leader. Sophocles, following Aeschylus' lead, introduced a third actor. The additions of these actors on stage enabled drama to become more complex. The playwrights were now able to depict open conflict between characters.

Structure of Classical Tragedies

Most Greek tragedies follow a similar overall structure. They begin with a *prologue* in which events that have taken place prior to the opening of the play are communicated to the audience. Following the prologue comes the parados, the highly ceremonial entrance of the chorus. The chorus usually has an opening speech in which their role in the play is introduced and they set the mood.

The chorus usually served a dual function. As times they chanted, sang songs, danced, told stories, and provided exposition. At others, though, they functioned as an actual character within the play, often engaging in dialogue with the other characters.

Following the parados, the rest of the play consists of a series of episodes divided by choral songs, known as stasima. At the conclusion of the play, the exodus is the final departure of all characters and the chorus from the stage.

The Theater Architecture

As dramatic festivals became more popular, permanent theater spaces began to be constructed. One such theater was the Theater of Dionysus in Athens. The main feature of the theater was the orchestra, or "dancing place." It was a large open area where the action primarily took place. Originally, the audience sat or stood on a slope facing the orchestra. Eventually, the *theatron* was added. The theatron, which means "seeing place," was a series of permanent rows of benches, in circular fashion, that rose above the orchestra. The final component of the Greek theater was the skene, which means "hut." The skene was a small building set back from the orchestra. While it was often used as a dressing room, the structure itself often acted as a setting for the play. This is why many Greek tragedies are set in front of a palace or tomb.

Record Your Notes Here

Your Notes Here

Suggested Notes

Classical Theater

The Origins of Tragedy

—Came from rituals to Dionysus = god of fertility, wine

—Aristotle's Poetics: trag. from dithyrambs = elaborate
  rites to D.

  —innovation by chorus leader, speaks in character

  —credited to Thespis

Festivals

—held in honor of D.

—City of Dionysia (CD) in Athens

Development of Tragedy

—534 B.C. = trag. officially recognized at CD

—6th c. = no remaining plays

—5th c. = 3 trag. playwrights

  —Aeschylus; adds actor 2

  —Sophocles; adds actor 3

  —Euripedes

Structure of Classical Tragedies

—prologue

—parados = chorus enters

  (role of chorus = sing, chant, also acts as character)

—episodes

—stasima (choral songs)

—exodus

Suggested Notes (Cont.)

The Theater
—Theater of Dionysus
—orchestra (dancing space)
—theatron (seeing place) = circular seats
—skene (hut) = dressing room/set in background

Reading Response

The right-hand column is the student's original response to the chapter. The left-hand column contains comments and questions she added later on in the semester when she read over her response.

READING RESPONSE: CLASSIC THEATER, CHAPTER 2

	I thought the chapter was dry; the information was just presented in a very straightforward way without much color. But I found that if I tried to imagine what theater was actually like in ancient Greece, it made the reading more interesting. It sounds like the theater of that period was really imaginative.
When we read about Japanese Noh theater, I again observed this connection between ritual and drama.	The author seems to emphasize the connections between religion and theater; he keeps showing how theater emerges from religious rituals. The orderly structure of the tragedies he describes did sound very ritual-like. I wonder what other aspects of Greek drama are similar to ritual. Today's theater is like a ritual as well—there's a definite order of events as well as a certain awe people feel for live theater. But I thought the Greek festivals sounded more like the Cannes film festival than religion. I'd like to get a

READING RESPONSE: CLASSIC THEATER, CHAPTER 2 (cont.)

	better idea of what exactly went on during those festivals.
	I've heard of those three tragic playwrights before, but I don't know much about them. I remember reading
In chapter 3, we read more on this. The addition of a second and third actor adds more conflict. It takes at least two people to have an argument, right?	Antigone in high school (which one wrote that? I think Sophocles). I know we're going to be reading more plays by these guys in class. I want to see exactly how they are different from each other. How much of a difference was made by adding that second and third actor?
We learned about Aristotle's theory of tragedy. Did Shakespeare follow this theory? I need to look into this.	The layout of the theater sounds cool. I tried to picture how it looked. It would be great to see a play in one of these theaters. They remind me a bit of what I heard about the Globe Theater where Shakespeare was first performed— people also sat in circles around the stage. I wonder if there are other similarities in the two theaters. Actually, I really wonder if Greek tragedy is similar to Shakespearean tragedy. The structure described in this chapter was certainly different from the structure of tragedies in Shakespeare.

Using Other Sources (Non-Textbooks)

So far we've primarily been discussing how to read textbooks. While many college and high school classes rely on textbooks, especially for introductory and survey courses, you will probably be assigned readings from a variety of sources. You can generally follow the reading strategy outlined above, although you may emphasize certain steps more than others, depending on the type of source.

These are some of the typical sources you might encounter:

Scholarly Articles

These are articles written by professors and academics that appear in professional journals. They are often only a few pages (between five and ten), but don't be fooled by their length; they will require much more time and effort to work with. These are the sources most likely to be written in academic style, using sophisticated vocabulary and addressing complex ideas. The authors of these articles often assume their readers have the same level of education and background as they do. That means they will be less likely to define key terms and concepts for you than a text book does. You therefore might have to spend more time in the library using other sources to explicate the information conveyed.

Primary Sources

Many courses include primary sources, such as historical documents, novels, plays, etc. It is vital that you read these sources before class so that you can follow the lecture. Primary sources, particularly works of literature, often won't involve key terms and won't necessarily include clearly identifiable introductions and conclusions. Rather than making outlines that include key terms, you need only to note the general themes. You should still write a reading response, as this will help you recall the source in more detail when you study for an exam.

LAB REPORTS

For science classes, you may be required to read laboratory reports, accounts of experiments, and scientific studies. The most important element to read and make a note of is of course going to be the outcome of the experiment. But don't be fooled into thinking you only need to read the conclusion. Make certain you have a sense of the general parameters of the experiment, such as the setup of the study and who participated in it. Also, try to evaluate the study: Are there any flaws in the setup or in the scientists' reasoning? Are there any factors that could have influenced the findings other than the ones the scientists discussed? What are the assumptions that

were made in the study? Were the scientists aware of these assumptions? These issues often form the basis for examination questions. On the other hand, many lab reports will include lengthy sections in which the writers review relevant articles and studies that influence their own methodology. Unless your professor tells you otherwise, it is probably not as important that you read this section as it is to read about and understand the nature of the particular study.

COURSE PACKETS

Sometimes the professor will put together a special packet for the course that includes a variety of materials such as articles, charts, diagrams, and excerpts from longer texts. Always read everything in a course packet carefully. If the professor took the time to make it up, it is probably important.

Sample of a Skimmed Textbook Entry

The following is a page from a chapter of a textbook. The highlighted sections indicate the parts you would read if you were skimming the chapter. As an exercise, try reading just the highlighted section. Do you still manage to get a general sense of the content of this chapter?

CHAPTER 1

Early British History and Culture

In this chapter, we will trace the early history of Britain, from the Anglo-Saxon conquest, circa 450, through the Norman Conquest in 1066. We will also explore the effects of these two invasions on British life, culture, and literature.

The Anglo-Saxon Invasion and the Heroic Ideal

In the first half of the fifth century, around the year 450, groups of people known as the **Anglo-Saxons** invaded the isle of Britain. At that time, Britain was inhabited by a group known as the **Celts**. This so-called invasion was the latest in a series of migrations that had started years before. These migrations involved a series of Germanic tribes from the northeast of Europe who moved into areas of the Roman Empire in the west, south, and southeast. The Anglo-Saxon invaders actually consisted of three tribes—**the Angles, the Saxons, and the Jutes.** Although they were independent, these three tribes shared a common Germanic heritage that helped unite them.

According to Germanic heritage, society was originally organized by the family unit. The head of the family was the **chief** of all his close kinsmen. As time passed, that social unit grew; numbers of families became united under a **king**, derived from the Germanic word for chief. However, the kingships still were relatively small and quite unstable. Thus, even after the Anglo-Saxons settled in Britain, the island was still broken up into many different, constantly shifting kingdoms.

Central to the kingship system was a notion of ideal kingly behavior that is generally referred to as the **heroic ideal.** Kings were supposed to prove themselves worthy of their leadership roles, particularly by showing their skill and courage in battle. These qualities when found in a king provided a sense of stability at a time when life was anything but stable. The heroic ideal also came to refer to the warriors who served the king and attempted to mirror his behavior and earn his favor. The Anglo-Saxons brought the heroic ideal with them to Britain and it became a part of English culture and tradition. As we will see, this heroic ideal is a central aspect of Old English literary works such as Beowulf.

The Norman Conquest

As we have seen, in the early half of the middle ages, the inhabitants of Britain lacked any kind of stable societal organization. That all changed in 1066, the year of the **Norman Conquest.**

In 1066, Britain was once again invaded by a Germanic tribe, but one very different from the Anglo-Saxons. These people were known as the **Normans,** and they were descendants of Scandinavian adventurers who had seized a wide part of northern France at the start of the tenth century. Although the Norman rulers' leader, **William,** was a subject of the king of France, Normandy was very much an independent entity. The invasion of England was led by William. Still largely divided, the English were easily overthrown at the **Battle of Hastings.** William's forces went on to take over England and he became its king.

UNDERSTANDING TROUBLESOME TEXTS

DIFFICULT TEXTS

As we mentioned before, many academic texts are difficult because they are written in a particular style featuring sophisticated language, long, complex sentence patterns, and intricate structural arrangements. This style can be very hard to understand, especially if you aren't used to it. The good news is that the more you read this kind of writing, the better you will get at understanding it.

In the meantime, there are several ways to help yourself along:

1. Put Up a Fight

The most important rule for learning how to read these texts is that you be willing to struggle with them. It's always easier to avoid a problem or a difficult situation by making excuses, but you don't gain anything that way. Don't give up reading a difficult text by making excuses like "this is boring" or "this is pointless" or "this is just too hard for me." Instead, go in fighting and put up a struggle. Acknowledge that a text is difficult and therefore may take more time and effort than usual. Take the attitude that even if you can grasp just a small portion of the text, it's better than nothing. You may even surprise yourself and pick up more than you thought.

If you want to make yourself feel good about a reading assignment, try this exercise. When you finish reading a difficult text, ask yourself, "What did I learn reading this?" and then take a few minutes to write down *anything* new you did learn, no matter how big or small it is. It may just be the names of a few important people, or it may be a whole new theory. When you're done, you'll see that even if you have not understood everything, you did in fact learn a great deal—things you would never have learned if you had given up right at the start.

2. Concentrate on the Big Picture

With many reading assignments, the whole is much more important than the various parts. But if you get caught up in each small section of a text, you lose sight of the big picture and don't really learn anything. Rather than trying to understand every word, line, and paragraph of a text, concentrate on getting the gist of it. Even if parts of a text are totally incomprehensible, the main points may still be crystal clear by the time you get to the end. Try to identify the themes of the text and keep them in mind as you read. If you come across difficult sections, see if you can figure out how they tie in with the main topic. When you are finished reading the entire text, ask yourself, "What were the main points of this text?" and take a few minutes to write them down. If you know what the main points are, you can still refer

to the text on exams—even if you haven't understood everything in it.

3. Only Look Up Repeated Words

A text may be difficult because it includes many words and terms you are unfamiliar with. Some of these new words will be key terms. Others will be sophisticated words typically used in serious academic texts but not in everyday conversation.

In making an effort to understand a difficult text, you may be tempted to look up the definition of every new word. That's going to take a lot of time; it's also going to disrupt the flow of your reading and make it harder for you to keep track of the general themes. You are therefore much better off *not* stopping when you see a new word. Continue to read and try to get the gist of the sentence or paragraph. Very often the context of a new word will be enough to help you get at least a partial sense of what it means.

At the same time, if any word is repeated several times, then you might want to look it up. Chances are this word is one commonly used in academic texts and worth knowing. But don't interrupt your reading to look up the word. You can make a note of it and look it up later. That way you won't disrupt the flow of your reading. Once you've looked up the meaning of the word you may want to go back to that section of the text and reread it. Try to learn at least one new word (that you look up in a dictionary) for every passage you read—but don't make yourself crazy by looking up every word.

4. Get Help

If you are having tremendous difficulty with a particular text, there's no reason why you can't seek help. Just as you do for your lecture notes, you can try to find other textbooks and source materials that cover similar topics. Go look at other textbooks, academic encyclopedias, study guides (such as Schramm's Outlines or Barron's Guides), and other books on the same general subject. Check the back of the assigned text to see if there is a bibliography or list of suggested reading.

You might get lucky and find a book or article that covers the exact same material but is written in much simpler language that makes it easier to understand. Even if you find sources that are equally complex, it will probably help to read them. Other

sources might describe the same material in a different way: They might use different illustrations and examples to describe the same overall principles. By reading more than one source on the same topic, you gain a fuller explanation and a more complete understanding of it.

WORK TOGETHER

You can also discuss the reading assignment with fellow students. Since these assignments are not graded, there's no reason why you can't work with friends. Perhaps a fellow student just happens to have a better understanding of this particular subject than you do, and you can ask questions. It's important, though, that you have a *discussion* with the student about the text rather than just get answers. Express your own opinions and thoughts. Having a conversation ensures that you listen carefully to the other student and also that you think more about the text.

Even if other students don't have a firm grasp on the material, a discussion may help you come to a better understanding of it. Try taking turns attempting to "teach" sections of the text to one another; very often, in the process of trying to explain something to another person, you also manage to explain it to yourself.

Finally, you can always ask your instructor for extra help. However, only do this if you really need the help. Don't ask for it on every assignment. You don't want to give the impression that you are too lazy to do the work and can't think for yourself. If you do decide to ask for help, see your professor during office hours or after class and say, "I'm having trouble understanding 'Source X.' I wonder if you can recommend some other sources to read that could provide me with more information." By asking for more sources rather than an explanation of the material, you are indicating that you are willing to work on your own. The professor then may, in addition to recommending sources, ask you where you are having trouble and offer further explanations. Whatever you do, do not complain about how hard or boring a reading assignment is—nothing makes a worse impression!

POORLY WRITTEN TEXTS

If you are having trouble with a text, it won't necessarily be because it is difficult; it may just be poorly written. Don't assume that just because a professor assigned a text it will be good. Many textbooks are mediocre in quality, sloppily thrown together,

written without much insight or concern for detail.

You should learn how to become a critic of the materials you are assigned to read. This means evaluating texts for yourself by reading them with a more critical eye. Have key terms been clearly defined? Is the text organized in a clear, logical fashion? Are there detailed explanations of important terms and concepts? Did the author provide detailed illustrations and examples to support various arguments, concepts, and points? Is information factually correct?

If you deem a particular text is poor, feel free to find alternative sources. Go to the library and check the subject catalog for other sources. If your assigned text includes a bibliography or suggested reading list, try to find some of these sources. They might be better written than the original text.

When you don't like the assigned textbook for your course, you can try to find another one. Check the library or a bookstore. There will usually be several textbooks available for a basic college course. You may even consider buying a second textbook to have on hand.

If you use an alternative source, make certain you compare it to the one your teacher assigned to see that the same general topics are covered. Compare the headings and key terms to see that the same topics are covered.

BE A SELECTIVE READER, NOT A SPEED-READER

Read This

Yes

Don't read this

This

Forget it.

Not this

Read

Not necessary

WHAT'S WRONG WITH SPEED-READING?

As we noted at the beginning of the chapter, you are probably going to have many more reading assignments than you can possibly read. For many students, the solution is to take a course, or buy a book, on speed-reading. However, speed-reading is perhaps the most passive form of reading there is. Most speed-reading

methods encourage you to flip pages as fast as possible by reading only small sections of the text, such as the middle column on the page. The advocates of these methods claim that you do, in fact, comprehend everything you read this way; and that as long as your eye sees words on the page, you can "read" them.

The problem with this method is that you don't have the opportunity to think about what your eye sees. And if you don't think about the material, you are not going to absorb it. That means it can be all too easily forgotten. You probably won't be able to use the assigned reading material to answer questions on an exam.

If you can't read everything you are assigned and speed-reading doesn't help, what can you do? The answer is to become a *selective* reader. Being a selective reader means making intelligent and informed decisions for yourself about what you can and should read. It means that although you may not read everything, you will think carefully about what you do read and learn from it.

SELECTIVE READING GUIDELINES

The most basic principle of being a selective reader is that you make educated decisions about what to read, what to cut, and what to skim. But you need to be smart. You don't want to ignore a source that is crucial to your understanding of the topic. You also don't want to cut a source you are likely to be tested on.

You need to at least glance through each source to get a sense of its contents, so that you can make an educated decision. Based on your sense of what is covered in the text, your time frame, and your previous knowledge of the topic, you can make decisions about what to read.

Here are some likely decisions:

- Read the entire text very carefully, just skim it, or ignore it completely.

- Read some sections of the text very carefully, and merely skim others.

- Only read sections of the text that are new to you; if sections rehash terms and concepts you already know about, skip them.

- Only read sections of the text that you know are relevant to the material covered in the course. For example, if you see sections that reflect things your professor has discussed in class or reflect topics listed on the syllabus, you probably want to read them.

- Rather than read all assigned texts for all of your classes, only read the most important texts for each course.

PRIORITIZE YOUR READING LIST

You might want to prioritize your reading assignments, starting out with the sections you deem most important or relevant. If you then find you have more time available, you can read others. If you see something your professor has previously mentioned, or something you know will be covered in class, that might be your priority. Similarly, you might want to prioritize things you don't know over things you are already familiar with.

In general, you should probably read primary sources over secondary sources. A primary source is a work written directly by the individual being focused on in that particular class, such as a playwright or novelist, a historical figure who wrote documents, treatises, theories, or scientists' and lab reports. A secondary source is anything written about a primary source, such as textbooks, journal articles, term papers, reviews. A primary source would be an article written by Freud; a secondary source would be an article *about* the article by Freud. Primary sources are usually more central to classroom discussion and lectures and are therefore more worth reading. You're likely to be lost in a class if you haven't read a primary source that is the topic of discussion. Questions about primary sources are also likely to show up on an exam.

While reading all primary sources should be a priority, it might not always be feasible. When you're in a bind, try to track down a source that summarizes a particular primary source. For example, there are several student guides to works of literature that you can buy in most bookstores. In the reference section of the library, you will also find various encyclopedias and dictionaries that summarize major works by major writers, scientists, historians, and theoreticians. However, you should only refer to these summaries and student guides if you are *really* pressed for time. Reading a summary never takes the place of reading the actual source. In fact, some summaries overlook important information and can give you a misleading impression about what is covered. If you use a summary, you should try to read the primary source sometime before the exam so you can be prepared to answer questions about it in detail.

In addition to evaluating which texts are most important to read for *each* course, you may also want to compare assignments *between* courses. Each week, look at the reading assignments for *all* your courses. You may decide to read the most important texts in each course and skim or ignore others. Or, you might find it is valuable to do all the reading for one particular course, while it is not necessary for others. Some professors rely heavily on outside reading assignments and assume students will keep up with the reading, while others consider reading secondary to the lectures. As the semester goes on, you will get a sense for how important your professor thinks the reading assignments are.

As you make decisions about what to cut, remember that you can always go back and read what you decided to skip. If, for example, you find that your professor discusses a text in detail during a lecture, you should probably read it carefully. Later, if you discover you have free time, or a week when the reading assignments are relatively light, you may want to use that time to catch up on previous assignments.

How to Skim a Text

Rather than not read a text at all, you may decide to skim it. Skimming a text doesn't mean you just read it at a slightly faster pace than usual. It is really a form of selective reading.

The best way to skim a text is to do the following:

1. Read Introductions, Conclusions, Summary Paragraphs

You should read the introduction and conclusion of each text in their entireties, as these paragraphs usually outline the most important points covered in the text. You might also look for "summary paragraphs." These are paragraphs within the text that summarize smaller sections of the text rather than the whole thing. If a text is divided into topics and subtopics, each with their own heading, these sections might have their own introductions and conclusions. As you skim, be on the lookout for terms like "in conclusion," "to sum up," and "therefore" that indicate the author is summarizing various points.

2. Read First and Last Lines of Paragraphs

If you go through a text and read just the first and last line of each paragraph, you will actually get an adequate concept of what the text covers. The first line of many paragraphs will introduce the topic covered, while the last line will often summarize the contents of the paragraph or serve as a transition to the next paragraph. As you read first and last sentences, you might come across a line that indicates a paragraph is particularly important or intriguing. If that happens, go ahead and read the entire paragraph.

3. Look at Illustrations

Just as first and last sentences of paragraphs often sum up key points, pictures, charts, and diagrams usually correspond to key information conveyed in the text. Look over all of these and read the captions that explain them.

4. Read All Words and Phrases That Are Set in Boldface or Italics

If the term is unfamiliar to you and seems significant, read the entire sentence as well.

REMEMBER THE BIG PICTURE!

The reading assignments you do for your classes are not isolated exercises. Each piece you read is a part of the bigger picture: the particular course or subject. It is also a part of an even bigger picture: your general knowledge. In fact, even the reading you do outside of class contributes to your general knowledge. You learn *something* from *everything* you read, whether it's a textbook, novel, or magazine article. Ask yourself what, exactly, you are learning from this piece? How is this text contributing to your overall knowledge? As long as you keep that big picture in view, you'll always be an active and effective reader.

Important Points to Remember

1. Be an active reader; become involved with what you read.

2. For each reading assignment, know where you're headed and why.

3. Think while you read and after you read; ask yourself questions and write a response.

4. Throw away the highlighters; rely on your own notes about reading assignments.

5. Be a selective reader rather than a speed-reader. Prioritize your reading assignments in order of importance. If you can't read the entire assignment, skim it.

6. Be willing to work hard on difficult texts; don't use the "boredom" excuse.

CHAPTER 4

Writing Essays

WRITING WRONG

The Right on the First Shot Writer

When the "First Shot" writer sits at her computer to type her essay, she's already spent the last few days conducting research and taking notes so she has a definite idea about what she wants to write. She is confident that her ideas are quite sophisticated and will certainly impress the teacher. Typing up the essay takes about three hours. Certain the essay is excellent, she prints it out and staples it together without reading it again. When she gets it back, she finds she got a C. The teacher had questions about almost every paragraph and seemed to have completely missed her brilliant ideas.

The Over-Researched Writer

The "Over-Researcher" spends about a month meticulously researching his essay topic. He takes out scores of books and articles from the library and takes pages of notes on all of them.

When he writes his essay, he makes certain to mention and quote from each and every source. However, rather than being impressed by all the research he's done, the teacher observes that there is not a single original idea in the essay. When the teacher meets with the student, she asks him, "What do you think about this topic?" and the Over-Researcher realizes he has no idea.

The Last Minute Brainstorm Writer

The night before an essay is due, the "Brainstormer" sits at her computer. Off the top of her head, she begins writing. As she works, she thinks of more and more things to say about the topic, and she continues to write them down. After writing several paragraphs, she thinks of something new that relates to her first point. She then writes, "By the way, in reference to my earlier point, I also believe . . . " and expands upon that point. She then starts writing about something else that occurred to her. She spell-checks the document, prints it out, and turns it in. When she gets it back, the teacher has circled the last sentence of the essay and written: "This is the most powerful and original idea in your essay. You should have started with this point and spent the entire essay addressing this idea. I would have given you an A."

Essay Checklist

Before turning in an essay, run down the following list of questions. If you make certain to do everything on it, you are more likely to turn in a quality piece of writing.

- Are my topic, thesis statement, and general approach clear to the reader?
- Have I proven my thesis statement beyond the shadow of a doubt?
- Have I made my argument fully and persuasively?
- Does every paragraph clearly relate to the thesis statement?
- Does every paragraph center on a single point that is clear to the reader?
- Do paragraphs and sentences flow together? Have I included transitions that connect sentences and paragraphs together?
- Have I supplied all the information a reader needs to understand all my points? Have I anticipated any questions a reader might have and included the answers?
- Have I cut out any excess words, sentences or paragraphs that don't contribute anything substantial?
- Have I varied my word choices?
- Have I altered my sentence patterns?
- Have I used all of the words correctly and in the right context?
- Have I proofread for grammar, spelling, and punctuation errors?
- Have I cited all quoted and paraphrased sections? Have I used the proper citation format? Have I included a bibliography written in the proper format?
- Have I printed out a clean, final copy? Is it double-spaced and stapled together? Does each page have a page number and my name? Have I included a title, my name, the course, and the date on the first page of the essay or on a title page?
- Have I made an extra copy to hold onto?

WRITING RIGHT: IT'S A BIG IDEA

Writing essays requires you to communicate back things you have learned. Both taking tests and writing essays center on how well you communicate.

Many people think writing is all about correct grammar and spelling. However, an essay can have flawless grammar and still not say anything. The essence of writing is communication. In any work of writing, you are communicating your ideas, thoughts, and beliefs to someone (or even yourself) in a way that makes them clearly understandable.

When you are immersed in writing an essay for class, you can easily forget that you are trying to communicate with a specific person—your teacher, who will grade the essay. However, you should always keep this in mind: *What can you write that will most impress your teacher?*

A teacher is probably not going to be overly impressed by flawless grammar and spelling; those qualities are expected. What will impress the teacher is the quality and strength of your ideas. As the above three examples

indicate, ideas are the crucial component of a good essay. They must be communicated in a manner that makes them accessible to the reader.

Coming up with sophisticated and intelligent ideas is your responsibility; no book can give them to you. However, this chapter can teach you how to communicate those ideas in such a way that will show them off to their advantage. This chapter outlines a step-by-step approach to writing essays that ensures your ideas are communicated in a clear, organized, and powerful manner.

A STEP-BY-STEP APPROACH

1. Choose a general topic.
2. Read, think, percolate.
3. Design a thesis statement.
4. Conduct research.
5. Take notes on sources.
6. Jot down your own ideas.
7. Organize your notes and plan an attack.
8. The three-part essay structure:
   — Introduction.
   — Body.
   — Conclusion.
9. Write the first draft
10. Revise and redraft.
11. The final edit.

1. Choose a General Topic

To a large extent, the topic you choose determines how the final product will turn out. After all, an original and exciting topic will more likely result in an original and exciting essay. You should therefore not choose a topic haphazardly.

Your choice of topic must take into account the nature of the assignment and its requirements. Sometimes a teacher will assign a very specific topic

and provide you with detailed requirements, specifying what the essay should address. However, even with the most rigidly defined assignment, you are going to have room to maneuver. In this case, the challenge is to view the subject from your own point of view and somehow to make it your own. You still need to spend time thinking about the assignment and how you plan to approach it in your own individual manner.

At other times, a teacher will suggest several topics or provide you with a very loosely defined assignment that gives you a great deal of freedom. Don't make the mistake of thinking that being allowed to choose your own topic makes the essay easier to write. Having free rein with an essay is exciting, but it is also overwhelming. There are so many possibilities for topics, how are you supposed to find one that's right for you?

WHAT INTERESTS YOU?

Choose a topic that, first and foremost, interests you. You are going to spend a great deal of time working on this essay, and if the topic itself doesn't ignite your interest, those hours will seem even longer and the writing process even more tedious. However, if you choose a subject you sincerely want to know more about, then the process of researching and writing the essay will be interesting and engaging.

Think about the various themes and topics that have been addressed in class, as well as the reading assignments you've completed. Was there a particular subject that you enjoyed learning about? Was there anything you only touched on in class that you wanted to know more about? Did you have an intense emotional reaction to anything? Do you have a particular opinion or point of view about a topic you'd like to express?

CONSIDER YOUR AUDIENCE

In addition to considering your own interests, you do have to consider the teacher's expectations as well. Good writers always direct their work to the proper audience. For example, you would write a letter requesting a job interview in an entirely different manner than a love letter. In the case of a school essay, your audience will be the teacher who assigned it and will grade it. Before you begin work, make certain you understand the assignment, are aware of the teacher's expectations, and know the exact

requirements for the essay. How much research should you be conducting? How long should the essay be? What format should you use? Is there anything specific you should include or address?

You might also want to choose a topic that your teacher will find unique. Many teachers become bored reading about the same topics over and over again; most will therefore welcome a paper written on something unusual. For example, if everyone else in the class is writing about a certain work of literature, then consider choosing a different one. Just make certain that your teacher is open to new ideas and atypical subjects. It may seem difficult to be original, especially if you are writing about a topic such as a historical event or literary work that has been discussed by others for centuries. However, the way you approach this topic can add a new twist to it that makes it seem original.

TOO LONG, TOO SHORT, OR JUST RIGHT?

In addition to considering your own interests and the instructor's expectations, consider the length requirements. Essays are meant to be detailed, in-depth studies of a particular subject. In order to write a solid, focused essay, you should choose a topic that can be addressed fully and comprehensively within the page requirements set by the teacher.

If you choose a topic that is too broad for the paper's length requirements, you will wind up writing about it in simplistic, superficial terms. You won't have the space to get into much detail, so the entire essay will remain on a broad and obvious level. For example, it would be difficult to write an essay on "The Poems of Emily Dickinson" in only six pages; you'd have to discuss each poem in one or two lines in order to get to them all. However, you could choose a more limited topic, such as a common theme in Dickinson's work, and address that in some depth.

Students often initially choose topics that are too broad because they are concerned about meeting the page requirements. At first, six or seven pages sounds like a lot to "fill up," so you might choose a huge topic to guarantee you have enough to write about. However, once you begin thinking about and researching your topic in depth, you'll find you have plenty of material. In fact, you may find you need to leave some material out.

Yet choosing a topic that is too limited for the page requirements is also a problem. If your topic is too narrow, you may find yourself bending over backwards to meet the page requirements. Your paper then will be wordy and repetitive. For example, it would be difficult to find enough original thoughts to express on a single Emily Dickinson poem in a twenty-five-page essay; you would probably run out of ideas after the first few pages and repeat the same points over and over. Your topic should be broad enough so that you can fill the essay with strong ideas that keep the reader engaged.

Of course, you may not be able to settle on a specific topic right at the start. However, you don't need to. It's fine to begin with a broad, general topic and then gradually narrow it down until you hit upon a topic appropriate for the length of your essay.

A PLACE TO START

Here is a list of general topics that would make a good starting point for researching an essay:

- A particular work of literature, article or text, or a body of works
- An author, person, or a particular group of individuals

- A historical period or event, or a contemporary news event
- A literary period or genre
- A scientific field or subfield, in either the general sciences or social sciences
- A particular issue or subject of debate, either historical or contemporary

All of the above are broad subjects that would take lengthy papers to fully examine them. However, they all make fine starting points for essays; you can choose one and begin to think and read more about it. As you do, you'll gradually be able to narrow it down to a topic appropriate for the length of your essay.

2. Read, Think, Percolate

After you've chosen a general topic, you need to immerse yourself in the subject matter by reading and thinking about it at great length. Doing this, you learn more about the subject and generate ideas to use in your essay. You also begin to narrow the general topic down to a more specific one.

Start by reading anything you can find that relates to your chosen subject. The reference section of the library is an ideal place to begin reading. You can, for example, consult a general encyclopedia to see if there is an entry relating to your topic. Make certain you pick a thorough, academic encyclopedia such as *Encyclopaedia Britannica, Encyclopedia Americana*, or *Collier's Encyclopedia*. You can also find many specialized dictionaries and encyclopedias that address specific fields. If you're having trouble finding a source, ask the reference librarian for suggestions.

Next, search the stacks of the library for general books on your topic. You can use the library's index (either the card catalog or a computerized index) and search according to the subject. Pick books that look promising and copy down their call numbers. All of the books related to that subject should be located in the same section of the library, so you can go to that section and browse. Select a few books that seem interesting and read sections of them. You don't necessarily need to read the entire book. For example, reading the introduction to a book on your topic may provide you with a great deal of information.

If you are writing an essay that centers on a specific text, such as a particular book or article, it is crucial that you reread that text several times. As you read, jot down any ideas that pop into your head that might make a contribution to an essay. Reading the text a few times may provide you with enough ideas to get started on your essay. However, if you find you are having difficulty, you may want to do some background reading to help you arrive at ideas of your own.

Don't expect the ideas to happen right away. The mind needs to let information percolate for a while. Soon, you'll begin making connections with things you've learned, forming your own opinions, and gaining insight into the material. As you continue reading, your ideas and interests will become more focused and defined, and you will be able to narrow down your topic. Although you don't have to concern yourself just yet with taking detailed notes, remember to make a note of any ideas that pop into your head.

3. Design a Thesis Statement

The key to any essay is its thesis statement. The thesis is the paper's central idea; it functions as the essay's backbone, holding together the various parts as a cohesive whole.

The thesis statement is not the same thing as your topic, although they are closely related. Your topic is a general subject that you've read and thought about to generate specific ideas. Based on that process, you should now be able to formulate a particular point of view about some aspect of the topic. This viewpoint, condensed into a single sentence that sums up the central idea of the essay, is your thesis statement.

Every essay should have a thesis statement and all ideas expressed in the paper should reflect it. Without the thesis statement, the essay is merely a random list of ideas, without any clear, definable point.

A thesis statement can simply be a sentence that presents the central topic of the paper. Starting with this basic statement results in a straightforward essay that summarizes aspects of the subject matter. A more effective thesis statement reflects a specific viewpoint or opinion about the subject matter; the essay, in turn, represents the detailed argument that supports this viewpoint. Most teachers prefer this kind of essay; they are interested in your own perspective, rather than a summary of factual information. The more original the thesis statement, the more original—and impressive—your essay will be.

Here are some sample topics and the effective thesis statements that might emerge from them:

Topics

- American Literature of the 1920s
- Modern Psychological Theories and Treatments
- The Cold War

Thesis Statements

- Most American literature of the 1920s depicts a growing anxiety regarding the dehumanizing effects of industrialization.
- Although dreams play a central role in both Freudian and Jungian theory, there are crucial differences in the ways in which dreams are interpreted.
- The foreign policy of the United States during the Cold War indirectly served to escalate domestic problems on American soil.

In order for a thesis statement to be effective, it should be specific and reflect your own ideas; it should also:

BE SPECIFIC

An effective thesis statement is not too broad or general; instead, it should say something very specific about your topic. By being very specific, a thesis statement ensures that the essay remains focused and does not veer off into unrelated territory that distracts the reader.

REFLECT YOUR OWN IDEAS

Most professors will be more impressed when you express your own thoughts and ideas rather then regurgitating someone else's. A more effective thesis statement will therefore be original and reflect your own outlook on the subject. Make certain the thesis is phrased entirely in your own words.

BE SOMETHING YOU BELIEVE

The body of the essay must make a convincing argument supporting the thesis statement. However, it is extremely difficult to present a solid argument supporting an idea that you don't actually believe is true. Moreover, if the thesis statement reflects a personal belief, the entire essay will bear the strength of your convictions. Don't work against the

Who Wrote It? What's It About?

Identifying Your Essay

You should always put a title on your essay, as well as your name, the course name and number, the professor's name, and the date. You can either do this on the first page of the essay, or on a separate title page. Ask your professor if she has a preference.

If you are putting this information on the first page of the essay, you should go down about one inch from the top and type the following information against the left margin, double-spaced:

Your Name
The Professor's Name
The Course Number and Name
The Date

Then skip another two lines and center the title of the essay above the first paragraph. Do not underline the title or put it in quotation marks.

If you are using a separate title page, all information should be centered on the page. Put your title about one-third of the way down the page. Skip two lines and write the word "By" followed by your name. Below your name, write the course name and number, your instructor's name and the date; skip lines between each piece of information and center each line on the page.

Titling Your Essay

Students often fail to put titles on their essays, but the title, which indicates the general topic, is an important component. It can also give the reader a first impression of the writer. Try to conceive of a title that conveys information about the essay but is also intelligent and witty. One effective strategy is to use a title and subtitle, separated by a colon. The title should be a short phrase or quotation; the subtitle that follows should be a longer phrase or a sentence that explains the essay's topic in more detail.

Who Wrote It? What's It About? *(cont.)*

Examples

Open for Business: The Portrayal of Commerce and Economics in the First Scene of Shakespeare's *Merchant of Venice*

"I'll Talk About Anything I Want to, George": Vying for Control of Conversation in Edward Albee's *Who's Afraid of Virginia Woolf?*

When writing titles, remember:

1. Capitalize the first letters of the first and last word

2. Capitalize the first letters of all words in the title except for articles, prepositions and conjunctions.

3. Never put the entire title in quotation marks. However, if there is a quoted phrase within the title, you should put that in quotation marks.

4. Never italicize the entire title. However, if you mention the title of a major work within the title, you should italicize that.

5. Never punctuate the title with a period.

grain and choose a thesis statement that you don't support.

BE SOMETHING YOU CAN BUILD A SOLID ARGUMENT TO SUPPORT

Your goal in writing the essay is to convince your reader that your thesis statement is an accurate one; you want to prove your viewpoint beyond a shadow of a doubt. Therefore, make certain you pick a thesis you know you can prove. When you actually begin conducting research, you may find you don't necessarily agree with it or that you can prove it. If this is the case, change the thesis statement.

BE A SINGLE, DIRECT SENTENCE

Most essays for academic purposes are limited in length; you probably won't have to write a book-length dissertation. You therefore don't need a long, detailed thesis statement. Make certain you can phrase your thesis statement in one sentence. If you can't do it in one sentence, it indicates you are unfocused and confused about your idea, or that you've chosen a thesis too ambitious to be proven in a single essay.

You may need to fine-tune your thesis statement. Until you've actually begun writing, it is fine to have only a general sense of your thesis. As you

conduct research and gain more knowledge of your topic, you'll continue to hone your thesis statement.

Once you have an idea of what your thesis statement will be, it's a good idea to discuss it with your teacher. This will make certain you are on the right track. Your teacher may also have suggestions on how to conduct research and organize the essay.

4. Conduct Research

There are essentially two kinds of essays: ones that require you to do research from outside sources, and ones that do not. Essays that do not require research focus solely on your own thoughts and ideas about a particular topic; those that include research utilize information from outside sources to explain and support your thesis. Your teacher will tell you whether or not you are expected to do research and include other sources in your essay. If the teacher doesn't tell you, then ask.

There are two kinds of sources: *primary* and *secondary*. Primary sources are any texts that are the focus of an essay, such as specific works of literature, historical documents, or essays and articles that present certain theories and philosophies. For example, if you are writing about some of

Shakespeare's plays, then *Romeo and Juliet* and *Hamlet* would be primary sources. If your essay centers on a primary source, you must make certain you read it in detail and take notes on it.

Many essays also incorporate secondary sources. These are books and articles by critics, historians, scholars, and other writers who comment on and address primary sources, as well as other topics and subjects. If your essay involves conducting research, you need to track down secondary sources that address your topic and take notes on them.

WHERE TO FIND POSSIBLE SOURCES

There are obviously many sources that address your topic. However, before you read them, you need to find them. Fortunately, there are several resources you can turn to for help in finding possible sources:

THE LIBRARY SUBJECT CATALOG

All libraries list their sources in a catalog, either on index cards or on computer. The entries are usually organized three ways: by author, title, and subject. If you have a specific source in mind, you can consult either the author or title entries to find out if the library has the source and where it is located. If you are merely looking for general sources, though, you can search according to the subject.

Most libraries organize their subject catalogs according to the standard list of subjects set by the Library of Congress, although some libraries have their own classifications. The library should have a subject list available for you to consult. Sometimes a subject will be divided into subcategories. Try to find whatever subject or subcategory most closely relates to your topic.

PUBLISHED BIBLIOGRAPHIES AND INDEXES

There are many published bibliographies and indexes that list books and other sources, such as academic journals and periodic articles, on a particular subject. These bibliographies compile citations for various books and sources. A citation is a listing for a particular source that includes key information about the book, such as the author, title, publisher, and often a brief summary of the source's content. Bibliographies and indexes will usually be located in the reference section of the library. To find a bibliography on your topic, you can either ask the librarian for suggestions or consult the subject catalog.

Lists of Works Cited and Bibliographies in Sources

Most academic books, essays, and journals include their own bibliographies, list of works cited, or suggested further readings. These listings provide sources you might read yourself as part of your research. Each time you read a new book or article, check the author's bibliography or notes to see if there is anything of interest. You can also check the assigned texts for your course.

Computerized Information Resources

Several of the indexes listed above, such as the *MLA Bibliography* and the *Reader's Guide to Periodic Literature,* are available via computer. Many libraries have computer monitors set up that

enable you to conduct on-line searches. You can instruct the computer to search for sources relating to a particular author, title, or subject, and the computer will put together and print out a listing for you. Libraries have different regulations for conducting on-line searches. Some might require that you meet with a librarian to learn about the system before you use it on your own. You might also have to sign up for time to work on the computer.

The Internet is a valuable tool for finding sources, provided you know how to use it and have access to it. If you have access to the Internet, either at home or at the school's computer center, you can surf the net to look for sources. Through the Internet, you can gain access to indexes and bibliographies, and also find entire articles from newspapers, magazines, and periodicals. There are now many published guides and books that include simple directions for using the Internet for a variety of purposes, including conducting research.

Keeping Track of Sources

Whenever you find a reference to a source you'd like to investigate, make a note of it. It is extremely important that you write down all relevant information: the author(s), title,

Cyber-Books: Basic Books on Using the Internet

There are currently many books on the market about how to use the Internet. Here is a list of some basic guidebooks that are particularly accessible for beginners.

The Internet Guide for New Users by Daniel P. Dern
The Internet Navigator by Paul Gilster
Everybody's Guide to the Internet by Adam Griffin
The Complete Idiot's Guide to the Internet by Peter Kent
Internet for Dummies by John Levine, Carol Baroudi and Margaret Levine Young
The Internet for Everyone by Richard Wiggins

Internet for School Work. The following two books are particularly useful for students, as they contain specific sections on academic uses of the Internet.
Internet 101: A College Student's Guide by Alfred Glossbrenner
The Internet for Teachers by Bard Williams

Reference Books. The following books list sites on the Internet. They can be quite helpful for finding information quickly and efficiently.
The Internet Directory by Eric Braun
The Internet Yellow Pages
The World Wide Web Yellow Pages

Computer Magazines. The following magazines include a wealth of information and special tips about using the Internet and other computer technology. You may want to flip through them in the library or bookstore, or even subscribe.

Internet World
Wired

Here are some of the major bibliographies that might be helpful in your search for sources.

GENERAL SOURCES
Books in Print
Essay and General Literature Index
Reader's Guide to Periodical Literature

ARTS, HUMANITIES, AND LITERATURE
Annual Bibliography of English Language and Literature
Humanities Index
MLA International Bibliography of Books and Articles on the Modern Languages and Literatures

BIOGRAPHY
Biography and Genealogy Master Index
Biography Index
Who's Who

HISTORY
Historical Abstracts
International Bibliography of Historical Sciences

CURRENT EVENTS
Facts on File
Newspaper Indexes (check for specific newspapers such as the *New York Times,* the *Wall Street Journal,* etc.).

SCIENCES
General Science Index
Social Sciences Index

publisher (for a book); volume and date (for a periodical or journal); or anthology name and editor (for an essay or article included in another work). This information helps you to find the source and is also necessary when you create your own bibliography.

You can keep this information in a notebook or on a legal pad. However, a particularly efficient way to organize this information is to make bibliography cards. Simply fill out a separate 3x5 index card for each source by including all the relevant publication information. The cards provide you with flexibility: You can arrange them in any order, such as alphabetical by author or rank of importance, and you can also group various cards together to make your research more organized. For example, if you are going to a particular library or bookstore to look for sources, you only need to bring those cards with you. Finally, the cards provide you with extra room to take brief notes that will help you find the source, such as the call number or general location in the library.

You can also write a brief summary at the bottom of the card that indicates the general focus of the source, as well as some of the relevant topics it addresses. You will encounter a great many sources in the process of conducting research; having these notes can help you distinguish among different sources.

It's a good idea to get in the habit of listing the source on each card in the correct bibliographic format (see section on Giving Credit that follows). By doing this, you ensure that you have all the required information on the card that you will need for your final bibliography. It can be a real pain to have to go back to the library at the last minute to get information on a particular source.

Sample Bibliography Card

Call Number:

PN2023.5
Stevens, Jay Q. Shakespeare on the Contemporary American Stage. New York: Publishers Press, 1995.
Location: General Stacks, Fifth Floor
Summary: Reviews and analyzes several contemporary U.S. productions of Shakespeare's plays, including photos.
—Specific productions include The Tempest and Troilus and Cressida.

TRACKING DOWN SOURCES

Once you've found out about a source, you then need to track it down. You should learn how to use the library to your advantage. Think of the library as your office while you research your essay. Take the time to learn your way around and feel comfortable there. Most libraries are rich in resources; you just need to find out what they are. You might consider taking a library tour or orientation; if there isn't one available, wander around on your own. You can always ask librarians for help—that's what they're there for.

Use the best library that is available to you. A college or university library will probably have a more extensive collection and better resources than a local public library. However, the main branch of the public library in most cities will have a large collection of sources and varied services.

The bulk of the library's resources consists of books that are shelved in the "stacks." If you are looking for a book, simply check the library's catalog (either on computer or cards) to find the call number. The first few digits of the call number will generally indicate the subject and general section of the library housing the book, while the last few digits indicate the specific book. Using the call number, you can find the exact shelf where a book should be located. You then just need to match the call number you've written down to the one on the spine to find the right book. If you aren't certain where to look, ask the librarian.

At most libraries, the public is allowed access to the stacks. You can freely look through the shelves for books you want to take out. At some, however, you will need to fill out a request slip with the call number and give it to the librarian. The book will then be retrieved for you.

Of course, a particular book is not always going to be on the shelf. It might be lost or taken out by someone else. If this is the case, go to the circulation desk and tell them which source you need. They can often tell you when the book is due back and put a hold on it so it will be reserved for you once it is returned. If the book is missing, they can place a search on it. Unfortunately, a book search is going to have limited results; if the book is missing, you should probably assume it is not going to be found and look for other sources.

If the library doesn't have a particular source, don't despair. Many libraries provide an interlibrary loan service. Ask at the circulation desk or in the reference library what you need to do to get a book through this service.

When a book is located in the reference section, you will not be allowed to take it out of the library.

Library Offerings: More Than Just Books

Many people think of the library as a kind of big warehouse for books. While it is true that a library's collection of books can provide you with a wealth of information, most libraries have a great deal more to offer. The following is a list of the many resources and services a library—particularly a college library—will offer.

Holdings
- Encyclopedias, indexes, dictionaries, bibliographies, almanacs and other reference guides
- Filmstrips, microfilm, microform
- Newspapers and magazines
- Academic journals
- Rare document archives
- Videotape and film collections
- Audiorecordings
- Slides
- Files of student theses and dissertations
- Maps and atlases

Resources and Services
- Typewriter or computer centers (for typing essays, etc.)
- Copy machines or copy services
- Audio/visual screening/listening facilities
- Language labs
- Quiet study lounges and cubicles
- Lockers
- Interlibrary loans
- Search for lost books
- Holds placed on books already taken out
- Computers with access to the World Wide Web
- Computerized catalogs and bibliographies

The Librarian. Librarians are the most vital resource in the library; they can provide you with a tremendous amount of help for just about any academic project you pursue. Ask them questions; that's what they're there for.

Any good library should offer some, if not all, of the above resources and services. It's a good idea to wander around your library or take a brief tour to find out exactly what the library offers. Then take advantage of it. If you use the library properly, its resources can make the job of being a student much, much easier.

You'll have to photocopy relevant sections or sit in the library and take notes on the source. The advantage, though, is that you know the books will always be there.

In addition to books, libraries house many other research materials, including magazines, newspapers, journals, videotapes, audiotapes, and maps. These materials are usually kept within their own rooms or sections. You can ask the librarian or check the library directory to find where these sections are.

Magazines, periodicals, and scholarly journals are sometimes bound together in volumes and shelved in the stacks. This is why bibliographies list a volume number in addition to the date of a particular periodical. However, due to the enormous space newspapers and magazines take up, as well as the problem of decay, libraries only keep them for a limited time period. After a time, many newspapers, journals, and magazines are transformed to microform. Through a special photographic process, the entire publication is miniaturized and transferred to film. There are several types of microform, including microfilm, which is a long strip of film that comes rolled up, and microfiche, which is a single, transparent sheet.

The microforms are usually kept in a separate section of the library. The catalog will usually indicate if a particular source is available on microform. You can then go directly to the microform room. Make certain you have the exact title and date of the source. Usually a librarian will have to get the microform for you.

As a result of the miniaturization process, the print on microforms is too small to read with the naked eye. In order to read it, you need to use a special monitor, which will probably be where the microforms are kept. There are usually a limited number of monitors and you will often have to sign up for one and wait. Ask the librarian to set you up and show you how to use it.

Since you can't take the microform out of the library, it is important that you either take careful notes or make a photocopy. Some specially equipped monitors enable you to make photocopies of different pages as they appear on the screen, but this can become expensive.

In addition to using the library, you can purchase books from bookstores. However, this can also be very expensive. Moreover, most bookstores will only have current sources and you may need ones no longer in print. You can check *Books in Print* to find out if a book is still published and who the publisher is. If you really need the book, you can call local bookstores or contact the publisher directly to order it.

You might also try asking your teacher for help. Most teachers have extensive collections of books in their field. Tell the teacher that you've tried on your own to find a particular source and that it is unavailable. If the teacher owns it, he will most likely be willing to lend it to you. At the very least, the teacher may suggest other places to continue searching for it.

5. *Take Notes on Sources*

When you've tracked down a particular source, glance through it to determine if it is relevant and can contribute significantly to your essay. Read the preface or introduction of a book, or the first few paragraphs of an article, and try to identify the main argument or viewpoint. Is it well written and accurate? Are the arguments well supported? Is the author well qualified?

If you decide a source might help, read it very carefully and take notes. Many of these notes will eventually become vital parts of the essay, so it is extremely important that you take

them carefully and accurately. Being organized with your note-taking will make the process of writing the essay easier later on.

WHAT TO TAKE NOTES ON

When you are reading a particular source, you may not be certain what to take notes on. Sources can be quite long; how do you know what is relevant and what isn't?

The most important things to look for are anything that supports your thesis statement. Essentially, you are looking for hard evidence that argues in favor of your thesis. However, you can also take notes on anything that relates to your general topic, since these notes will help you develop a broad background knowledge of the field and might be used in the essay. Also, take notes on anything that intrigues you or sounds interesting. You won't necessarily use all of these notes in the essay. However, it is much easier to take notes and throw them out later than have to reread sources.

In the initial stages of research, you may not have formulated your thesis entirely or conceived of the overall points your essay will make. You therefore may be uncertain about what notes to take. It can be helpful to read a sampling of the sources you've tracked down before beginning to take notes. This will enable you to develop a background knowledge in the subject, which in turn will help you fine-tune your thesis. When you have a better idea of the shape of your essay, you can then go back to various sources, read them carefully, and take notes.

By the way, if your essay utilizes primary sources, you need to read these carefully and take notes on them as well. Notes and quotations from primary sources are particularly strong pieces of evidence, especially if a primary source is the focus of your essay.

HOW TO TAKE NOTES

There are two types of notes: *quotations* and *paraphrases*. A quotation restates a passage or a part of a passage from a source in the original writer's *exact words*. A paraphrase, on the other hand, restates the ideas in a passage rephrased in *your own* words.

When you are reading a source and come across a sentence or passage you think is relevant, decide whether you want to quote it or paraphrase it. You should generally paraphrase more often than you quote. It is too tedious and time-consuming to copy down long passages word for word. However, if a sentence or passage is written in a particularly interesting or powerful manner that you think will

stand well on its own in the essay, then copy it as a quotation.

Be certain you put the lines in quotation marks. To be certain you remember that the note is a quotation, you may even want to write "Quotation from Original" next to the line in parentheses. If you want to leave out part of a quotation because it is not relevant, you can use an *ellipsis* to indicate a word or phrase has been deleted. An ellipsis consists of either three spaced periods if the omission is within a sentence, or four spaced periods if the omission comes at the end of a sentence.

Sometimes, when you take a quotation out of context, it won't make sense on its own and will need some clarification. If you decide to add a word or phrase to the quotation, you must put it in brackets to indicate that the addition is not part of the quotation.

If you decide to paraphrase the source, you must rephrase it *completely in your own words*. Make certain that your paraphrase is an accurate restatement of the passage.

Occasionally, you will want to quote a few words or a particular phrase within a paraphrase. You can paraphrase the gist of the passage and include only a few words and phrases in quotation marks. For example, if the author has coined a particular term or described something in a unique way, you can quote those words exactly.

Examples of Quotations and Paraphrases

Original Source
"More often than not, American productions of Shakespeare's plays in the 1990s have relocated the setting and changed the time period from the original, ranging from a version of *Richard III* set in Italy under Mussolini, to a futuristic version of *The Tempest* set on a faraway planet. At best, these relocations serve to enhance and expand the plays' inherent themes; at worst, they are flashy gimmicks that serve to obscure and confuse."

Quotation in Notes
"More often than not, American productions of Shakespeare's plays in the 1990s have relocated the setting and changed the time period from the original . . . . At best, these relocations serve to enhance and expand the plays' inherent themes; at worst, they are flashy gimmicks that serve to obscure and confuse."

Paraphrase in Notes
Productions of Shakespeare in the 1990s change the scene or time period. Sometimes the change is positive and adds something, but at others it only makes things confusing.

Partial Paraphrase with Partial Quotation
Productions of Shakespeare in the 1990s change the scene or time period. Sometimes the change can "enhance and expand" the original themes; at others, the changes are "gimmicks" that "obscure and confuse" the theme.

Whenever you take quotes from a source, and even if you paraphrase them, you need to note the source and its exact page number(s). It is important that you do this carefully, as you must include this information later in the essay. If you don't acknowledge the original source, you are committing *plagiarism*, which is considered a serious breach of ethics that can get you expelled from school.

Keep careful records with complete publication information of all your sources. In order to credit the sources, you need to place a bibliography at the end of your essay that includes all this information. Again, using bibliography cards is the most efficient way to keep track of sources.

There are many ways to take notes. The simplest method is to use a notebook or legal pad as you read. Remember to indicate clearly which source the notes come from and their page numbers.

However, if you are utilizing many sources and taking many notes, the material can become difficult to manage. A more efficient and organized means of taking notes is to use notecards. These give you more flexibility—you can shuffle and reorganize them into various groups, or put aside those you decide not to use.

As you do with bibliography cards, take notes on index cards (you may want to use a slightly larger size, such as 4x6, so you can fit more notes). On each card, write down a particular piece of information from one specific source. Each card should contain a single, specific idea. Copying lengthy quotations and paraphrasing large chunks of text take away the flexibility that notecards provide you with in the first place. Try to limit each card to a single point.

As long as you have made a bibliography card, you don't need to put the full title and complete publication information on each notecard. Simply copy down the last name of the author in the upper left-hand corner of the card. If you are using more than one source by a particular writer, you can write down the author's last name and a key word from the title. In the top right-hand corner, write down the exact page number from which the noted quotation or paraphrase comes.

To ensure that you distinguish between quotations and paraphrases, you may want to write on the card in big, block letters "QUOTATION" or "PARAPHRASE."

Sample Notecard

> Stevens, Shakespeare   p. 42
> Productions of Shakespeare in the 1990s
> change the scene or time period. Sometimes
> the change is positive and adds something,
> but at others it only makes things confusing.
> (PARAPHRASE)

6. Jot Down Your Own Ideas

Regardless of whether or not you are required to conduct research, the heart of the essay should be your own ideas. When no outside sources are included, the assumption is made that the entire essay represents your own thinking.

However, even when the essay includes other sources, they should only serve to support your ideas.

Jot down your ideas before you actually begin writing the essay. In the course of researching and thinking about your topic, you will develop certain ideas and a sense of the major points you want to make. However, these ideas will still be in your head, where they are probably mixed together. In order to be a compelling, powerful essay, these ideas need to be organized in a logical manner. You need to get them out on paper, so you can examine them and plan a strategic way to address them in the essay.

Additionally, the writing process is like brainstorming; as you write about one particular idea or point, you'll probably find yourself conceiving of many additional ones.

You don't need to worry about things like grammar, spelling, format, or structure when you write down your ideas; you don't even have to write in complete sentences if you don't want to. Just write anything that comes to mind in relation to the topic. You can then refer to these notes—along with any notes from additional sources if this is a research paper—as you organize your essay.

When you are finished jotting down your ideas, read them over and transfer the major ones onto notecards. You can play around with how you organize them in this form, and also integrate them with the notecards from outside sources.

Sample Notecard of Original Ideas

My Idea for Essay

Cycles and Repetitions in LDJ.
There are lots of images that are repeated throughout Long Day's Journey.
— family mealtimes
— cycle of time; one day after another (implied in the title)
— drinking from the bottle then filling with water
— men leaving Mary alone on-stage

7. Organize Your Notes and Plan an Attack

Before lawyers go to court, they carefully prepare how they intend to present their evidence. They think about the order in which they plan to call up witnesses and the particular lines of questioning they will follow. Planning ahead this way guarantees an organized and strategically effective presentation of the case. Your essay similarly represents an argument—this one in support of your thesis. You also need to plan ahead, organizing your evidence and devising a presentation strategy.

The first thing to do is read through and evaluate all your notes—having notecards makes this especially easy to do. Decide which notes are necessary for your argument. *Everything in the final essay must relate to the thesis statement.* You may wind up putting many unrelated notes aside; don't let this bother you. By evaluating notes in a critical manner, only the most powerful material remains. Information that doesn't contribute significantly weighs down the essay and detracts from the more powerful ideas.

After you've weeded out the notes, read through the remaining cards a second time, this time grouping those that seem to belong together, such as notes that make a similar point or relate to the same issue. You can begin by separating them into very broad categories and then subdividing them into more specific groups. Each group should eventually center on a major point that you plan to make in the essay. As you work, keep your own ideas in mind. You may want to use them as the basis for grouping together the notecards.

Write a key word or phrase to describe each category on index cards to identify each group. If a card seems to belong in more than one group, place it in the one that seems most applicable; however, write a note on the card indicating other categories it relates to.

After going through your notes, you'll be sitting with several piles of notecards made up of various categories and subcategories of notes. Each group represents a point you plan to make in the essay. You need to decide next on the order in which you will address these points.

In planning your essay, it helps to make a rough outline. The outline simply lists the major points of the essay, and the smaller topics and issues that relate to each one, in the order in which you plan to address them. This gives you a clear map to follow when you sit down to write. Like all good maps it will keep you from getting lost. You'll be able to write in an efficient and organized manner, without worrying that you're straying from the main point.

Try to include as much detail as possible within the rough outline. The more specifics you include, the more organized you'll be. Beneath the general categories in the outline, you can mention specific notes from sources you plan to use; you might even want to write out or sum up specific quotations.

When organizing your points, make certain that you order them in a logical fashion. You want one point to lead to the next, so that the reader will be able to follow your argument without having to fill in gaps. Certain categories of notes should follow one another. For example, if you are going to argue against a particular theory, you first need to describe the theory. Similarly, if you are analyzing the causes of a historical event or charting developments in a particular writer's or artist's work, it will be important to raise the points in chronological order. Also, if you are comparing and contrasting two particular works, discuss them in sequence.

The order in which you raise points can influence the effect they have on your reader. In evaluating your different notes—your pieces of "evidence"—you've probably become aware that certain ones are much more powerful than others. Consider how to order your points so that the most persuasive ones pack the most punch. Strategically, you may want to build up to your most powerful point so you make a strong last impression on your reader. At the same time, you don't want to start off with a weak point that will make a poor first impression.

The strategy of your essay is a personal decision. Different writers have their own favorite strategic devices and techniques. Additionally, each essay has its own specific strategy and logic. Before you start writing, consider the overall effect you want to create and conceive of a strategy that achieves it.

Remember that this rough outline is not written in stone; you can make changes at any time. In the process of writing the essay, or after you've read over early drafts of it, you may find that certain points work better if addressed in a different place. You can make as many changes as you like, provided that everything in the essay still relates to the thesis.

8. The Three-Part Essay Structure

Before we talk about the actual process of writing an essay, we need to identify and discuss its overall structure. Although there are many ways to structure an essay, the most basic one is the three-part structure that includes an introduction, body, and conclusion.

It is not a law that you have to use this structure for everything you write. You might, for example, have a teacher who is open to more loosely

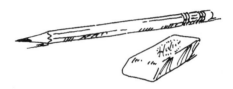

structured essays and who encourages you to be creative. However, this structure is generally the most effective way to write an essay for school. It ensures that the essay remains focused on a specific point and that ideas are presented in a logical and organized fashion. Following this structure, especially when you are first learning how to write academic essays, will help you write more persuasively.

THE INTRODUCTION

The introduction, at the beginning of the essay, is where you introduce your general topic, specific thesis statement, and approach or methodology. For most essays, the introduction only needs to be a single, well-written paragraph. (In bigger projects, ones that are more than twenty pages, such as an honors thesis or dissertation, the introduction can be somewhat longer.) By being succinct, the introduction has more impact.

You want the introduction to draw your reader into your argument right away. It functions somewhat like a movie preview, to give your audience a taste of what's to come, but not the whole story. You want your reader to be enticed and interested in what you have to say.

As the thesis statement is central to the essay, it is an important part of the introduction. However, you generally can't begin an essay with the thesis statement itself, because it represents a specific point of view about a broader subject. The introduction sets up the thesis by presenting general background information that gives it a context.

You should therefore begin the introductory paragraph with a broad, general statement about the paper's topic. Remember that the first few sentences give the reader the first impression of your essay; it is extremely important that you make a good first impression. The first sentences should be well written, interesting, and, most important, give the reader some idea of the paper's topic. The rest of the introduction then bridges the opening statement with the thesis statement, which is usually the last sentence of the introduction. You should indicate how you plan to approach your argument and the kinds of sources that will serve as your evidence. If you plan on looking at specific examples to prove the thesis, you can identify these cases also.

The introduction is the first and possibly only place in the essay where you spell out the thesis statement directly for the reader. You therefore need to be careful about how you word it. You don't want it to be too fancy, flashy, or wordy; the power of the idea should be enough to impress the reader. Just state it in a direct, unambiguous manner.

The introduction should come entirely from you. In general, it is not the place to quote and paraphrase outside sources. Those sources belong in the body of the paper, where you use them to prove the thesis statement. It wouldn't make any sense to discuss such specific sources before you've even stated the argument of the essay. Moreover, you want the reader to be primarily impressed by the power of your own ideas.

Here is an example of a standard introduction, beginning with a broad general statement and building up to the thesis statement:

Eugene O'Neill's <u>Long Day's Journey into Night</u> unfolds on a single day during which the entire history of the Tyrone family is revealed. Without ever disrupting the confines of the single day time frame and single room setting, O'Neill gradually reveals everything about the family members, from the troubled state of their present relationships to one another to their complicated and painful past histories. While many of these revelations are made in the characters' conversations, a detailed analysis of the play's structure reveals the central role it plays in emphasizing one family member's complicated relationship to another. O'Neill's masterful structure of the play particularly exposes the intricate family fabric and how it is grounded in a complex network of blame, denial, and deceit.

> Begins with a broad statement; introduces topic.

> Indicates way in which writer plans to approach the topic—through a detailed analysis of a single work.

> Thesis statement.

The above paragraph is an example of a standard introduction. You can, however, vary this format in different ways. Although the introduction is not the place to introduce specific secondary sources, you can open an introduction by summarizing a critical trend or issue that you discovered in your research. You can then indicate how your argument either compliments or counters that viewpoint or trend.

You can also occasionally begin an essay with a quotation from another source or by mentioning a specific source; however, you should only do this if the quotation or source is obviously connected to your thesis statement. If the quotation or source introduces specific issues, you probably should not raise it this early in the essay.

If you want to be a bit more creative with the introduction and you think your teacher is open to this kind of writing, you might start the essay with a brief anecdote or observation that connects with your topic.

Just remember that the introduction should always alert the reader to your general topic, your approach or methodology, and your thesis statement.

THE BODY

The body is the bulk of your essay; this is where you present your detailed argument that supports the thesis statement. After having conducted research and thought at length about your topic, you should have several points to make. You will therefore use the body to present your ideas in as clear and organized a fashion as possible.

If you have conducted research from primary or secondary sources, you can quote and paraphrase from these sources extensively. Information that comes from other sources serves as strong evidence. However, you should also take care to distinguish your own ideas from those in other sources. Quotations and paraphrases should only be brought into the essay to lend credence to your ideas. Whenever you introduce information from another source, you should explain exactly how it fits in with your own point. And always make certain that each time you quote or paraphrase an outside source, *you formally credit the source*.

There are three important components of a well-written body:

1. Material Clearly Relates to Thesis Statement

The most important thing to keep in mind when writing the body is that every bit of information you include should relate to the thesis and you must spell out exactly how it does. If something doesn't relate to the thesis, get rid of it; it's only clouding up your argument and detracting from its power.

2. It's All Down on Paper

Because your ideas make sense to you, you may think you have fully explained them, when in fact you haven't done so in a manner that someone else can understand. The reader cannot see inside your head. You must therefore explain all your points carefully, making than clear to the reader. Don't worry that you are over-explaining your points and ideas. It may seem that way to you, but a reader will need a detailed explanation in order to see your points as clearly as you do.

3. Flows Smoothly

As the writer of the essay, it's your job to act as the guide for the reader. As you ease the reader through the complexities of your argument, journeying from one point to the next, you want to create as smooth a path as possible, so that by the end of the essay, the reader won't feel disoriented. At times, you need to make it clear exactly where the essay is heading or summarize what has already been demonstrated. You also don't want the paper to be choppy or difficult to read. Instead, one idea or point should flow smoothly into the next.

One way you can ensure the paper is clearly organized is by focusing each paragraph around a specific point. The body should always be written in paragraphs, not in one long chunk of text. Each paragraph should focus upon a specific point, and every sentence in that paragraph should relate to it. Any sentence in the paragraph that doesn't should be taken out. It's also a good idea to begin each paragraph with a topic sentence that generally introduces the subject matter or main idea of the paragraph. The topic sentence can also serve as a transition between ideas, demonstrating how the next paragraph builds on, contrasts, or departs from the previous one.

If you've been working with notecards and a rough outline as suggested here, it will be easier to create a focused paragraph. Each grouping of notecards you created became a section in the rough outline. Those rough outline entries became the central points of individual paragraphs. See how simple this is?

Example of a Well-Structured Paragraph

Topic sentence builds on previous paragraph and introduces main idea of this paragraph. Despite the carefully contrived way O'Neill structures the play in order to present various combinations of characters on stage together, he maintains the play's highly realistic frame and maintains the illusion that we are witnessing one day in the life of the family. We see the characters go about their business, and we occasionally see them on stage with one other character in the living room, but never in a contrived manner that makes us too aware of the playwright at work. Characters leave the room to do what they normally would on any given day. For example, in the first act, Edmund goes upstairs to get a book, Jamie and Tyrone go outside to work on the hedge, and Mary supervises Bridget in the kitchen. We thereby have the opportunity to see each character alone with the others, but always in an appropriate mode that stays within the play's realistic constraint. In fact, this structuring enhances the play's realism. With many different interactions taking place within the living room, and with so much movement in and out of the room, O'Neill gives the impression that this is a typical day in the life of a real family.

Each sentence and paragraph in the body should flow smoothly and logically from one to the next. By adding transitional words and phrases in certain sentences, particularly topic sentences, your reader can easily follow how different points are related to one another.

There are many transitional words and phrases you can use to connect various sentences and paragraphs, including these:

- To build upon a previous sentence or paragraph: *and, also, additionally, as a result, consequently, further, furthermore, in addition, moreover*

- To compare with a previous sentence or paragraph: *similarly, in the same manner, likewise, at the same time, by the same token*

- To contrast with a previous sentence or paragraph: however, but, in contrast, nevertheless, although, yet, on the other hand

- To summarize or draw a conclusion: therefore, in other words, in short, to sum up, thus

THE CONCLUSION

After reading the body and all the evidence you've presented in support of the thesis, the reader should now view the thesis statement not as conjecture but as proven fact. That's exactly what you express in the conclusion. The conclusion is essentially the mirror image of the introduction, but one that stresses the fact that the thesis has now been proven. The conclusion should therefore refer to the thesis statement in some form, and affirm that it has been proven. You should also recap the major points you've made in the

paper to establish your argument.

Like the introduction, the conclusion for most essays only needs to be one paragraph and it should primarily represent your own words and ideas. This is also not a place to quote or paraphrase extensively from secondary sources.

Remember that, while the introduction contributes to the reader's first impression of your essay, the conclusion will influence the reader's final impression. You want to end with a bang—with some of your most powerful and dramatic writing—that leaves the reader absolutely convinced of the validity of your argument.

The most basic conclusion inverts the structure of the introduction, starting off with a restatement of the thesis statement, followed by more general statements that sum up the essay's main ideas. The final sentence is a broad remark about the subject or topic.

Here is an example of a standard conclusion:

Eugene O'Neill therefore structures <u>Long Day's Journey into Night</u> to emphasize the various tensions and problems within the Tyrone family. By alternating scenes of the whole family on stage with episodes of smaller groupings of characters, O'Neill exposes how much remains unspoken and unaddressed by the family unit as a whole. He also exposes the complex web of blame, deceit, and denial that exists beneath the family's seemingly normal exterior appearance. The structuring of the play also dramatizes aspects of the characters in dialogue, such as the men's continual abandonment of Mary and Edmund's propensity to stray from family conflict. <u>Long Day's Journey</u> therefore demonstrates the vital role the form of a play serves in enhancing the theme and content.

Restates thesis

Restates main points in the essay

Concludes with final broad remark

You can vary from this standard format. Many writers, for example, choose to introduce some new point or question in the conclusion that emerges from the thesis. After establishing the validity of the thesis statement, they then address its consequences or implications. Depending on the freedom your teacher allows you, you might also try to be more creative in the conclusion. No matter the form of the conclusion, the same general rule applies: The conclusion should bring the essay to a formal close and affirm that the thesis statement has been proven.

9. Write the First Draft

One of the hardest aspects of writing an essay is getting started. Even after all the research, it can be very intimidating to sit down and start writing. Part of the difficulty comes from the way we tend to view writing. We don't think of writing as a process, and only value the finished product— which is supposed to be flawless. This thinking places tremendous pressure on you; you think the writing needs to be perfect, and often you freeze up with panic, afraid to commit yourself to a single word on paper.

Good writing takes time and effort to produce. You can't expect to get the essay right on the first try and, in fact, you shouldn't even try. Instead, it's better to write in stages, making changes and improvements with each draft.

Correct grammar and spelling are important parts of an essay because they help make it understandable and readable. However, don't concern yourself with this in your first draft. The most important task is to get all your ideas on paper and to integrate them with notes from other sources. This eliminates a great deal of the stress about writing; you don't have to think about the "rules" at first and can simply concentrate on conveying your ideas.

Start at the beginning of the rough outline and simply start writing. Do your best to explain each of the points. As you need to, refer to your notecards and include quotations or paraphrases from other sources. Make certain you add citations for each sentence that include information from another source. Keep on writing until you've reached the end of the rough outline. Don't stop to go back or make changes. If you hit a roadblock, a point when you freeze and don't know how to proceed, mark the place with an X and move on to another point. You can go back to the trouble spot later.

This first draft will be extremely rough; the writing will be choppy and difficult to read. But that's okay—it's only the first draft and you are the only one who has to see it. This draft provides you with the raw material for your essay; you can then work on it and refine it until it is a real gem.

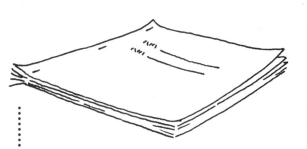

10. *Revise and Redraft*

Once you have completed the first draft, you should go back to the beginning and read it. Try to read it from an objective standpoint, as if you are someone else reading your work. Because you are so closely tied to your ideas, it will be difficult at first to be objective. Try to think of yourself as an editor going over an article by a reporter. As an editor, it's your job to make certain that everyone will be able to understand the article. You might also try reading it out loud, to listen to how it sounds.

As you read over the draft, ask yourself:

- Is everything explained fully?
- Will the reader understand everything as it is currently explained here?
- Are there any holes or gaps in the argument?
- Are any ideas not fully developed or partially explained?

Cite Specific: In-Text Citations, Footnotes, Endnotes, and Content Notes—What's the Difference?

Whenever you quote or paraphrase from another source, you must somehow indicate the name and page number of the original source. This is called a citation. There are several different kinds of citations, including in-text citations, footnotes and endnotes.

In-text citations, as the name indicates, are found within the body of the text, immediately after the sentence or section that has been quoted or paraphrased. They are usually placed within parentheses just before the period. The in-text citation is an abbreviated form of the source; it always corresponds to a more extensive listing in the bibliography at the end of the text. Although their specific ways of presenting information differ, both the MLA and APA formats recommend using in-text citations.

EXAMPLE OF AN MLA FORMAT IN-TEXT CITATION
The fog is the central symbol in Eugene O'Neill's *Long Day's Journey Into Night* (Alberts 42).

Footnotes and endnotes, more traditional forms of citation, are citations not found within the body of the paper. Instead, a footnote is located at the bottom of the page, and an endnote is put at the end of the entire paper. Within the text, a raised numeral following the passage that corresponds directly to a footnote or endnote that includes source information about the quotation or paraphrased. The notes are numbered consecutively throughout the paper.

EXAMPLE OF A FOOTNOTE OR ENDNOTE

In the text:
The fog is the central symbol in Eugene O'Neill's *Long Day's Journey Into Night*.[1]

Bottom of the page or end of text:
[1]Mark Alberts, *Eugene O'Neill's Flair for Symbolism* (New York: Publications Inc.) 42.

Cite Specific: In-Text Citations, Footnotes, Endnotes, and Content Notes—What's the Difference? *(cont.)*

Content notes resemble footnotes or endnotes, but they are not citations (they can only be used when in-text citations are already employed). Content notes provide additional information or explanations of what has been discussed in the body of the paper. For example, there might be certain material you wish to include that, while relevant to your essay, would disrupt the flow of it if included. Content notes are often used to elaborate upon or evaluate a source, to provide additional background information, or to take issue with a specific critic or researcher and thereby distinguish your own point of view. However, they should be used sparingly; too many content notes can make the paper confusing for the reader and overshadow the power of your own argument.

EXAMPLE OF A CONTENT NOTE

In the text:

The fog is the central symbol in Eugene O'Neill's *Long Day's Journey Into Night* (Alberts 42).[1]

Bottom of the page or end of text:

[1] I agree with Alberts that the fog is the most prominent and prevalent symbol in the play; however, it is also worth noting, as Susan Peters writes in her essay, "More than the Fog," that the fog functions along with other symbols in the play, such as the fog horn, wedding gown, and bottle of liquor, which are dependent upon one another to convey symbolic meaning.

- Does one idea flow smoothly into the next?
- What additional information does the reader need to appreciate this point?

Make appropriate notes. Try to anticipate specific questions a reader might have and write them down in the margins.

Now you are ready to go back to the beginning and rewrite. As you rewrite, answer the questions with more information. Revise the essay as many times as necessary, until you are satisfied with it. You make changes that improve the essay with each draft.

The first few times you read and rewrite, you should focus on the content—the ideas and points that are explained in the essay. Make certain all your ideas are clearly and fully explained—that nothing is ambiguous or partially stated, that there are no gaps in the discussion. Examine the organization of the essay and make certain that one point flows smoothly and logically into the next. You might try moving sections of the essay around to see if they work more effectively somewhere else. Check that everything in the essay supports the thesis statement, and take out anything that detracts from the argument.

In later readings, you can concentrate less on the content and more on the writing itself. Pay attention to grammar and to how things are phrased. Work on individual sentences and paragraphs to ensure they are well written and flow together. Think about ways you might rephrase or reword various sentences to make them clearer or more effective.

When you are finished with your essay, check to make certain you have met the page requirements set by your teacher. Remember, choosing the right topic from the start is the best way to ensure your essay will be the appropriate length. However, once you've started writing, you may find your essay is a bit longer or shorter than you intended. If your essay is only half a page or so longer or shorter, most professors will still accept it. However, if it is off by more than half a page, then you need to make adjustments.

If the essay is too long, read through it looking specifically for sentences and paragraphs that don't contribute a significant point to the essay. Examine all the points you've made to support the thesis, pick out whichever one is weakest, and cut out that section of the paper. You can also look for any sections of the paper that needlessly summarize or repeat points that are already quite clear for the reader. Just be certain whenever you make large cuts that you reread the entire essay to see that it still flows smoothly and makes sense.

If the essay is too short, then reread the entire piece looking for any sections that can be developed in more detail. Once again, ask yourself what questions a reader might have while reading the essay that you can answer within the text. You also might try to think up additional examples or illustrations you can add to the paper to support major points in more detail. As a last resort, you can look for additional quotations from outside sources you can integrate into the paper as a way of making it longer. Just make certain you discuss the quotations you include; if you just sprinkle them throughout the essay, it will be obvious to the professor that you are merely padding the essay with unnecessary material.

11. The Final Edit

After you have revised the essay several times and are generally satisfied with it, you edit it. Read the essay slowly and carefully for grammar, punctuation, and spelling errors. Examine each word, sentence, and paragraph. Have resources close at hand, such as a dictionary or grammar handbook, so you can check anything you are not certain about. It's easy to misuse a particular word or to confuse similar words; it's also easy to have a sense of what a word means but have the wrong context for it. You should therefore double-check the definitions of any unfamiliar or complicated words. The same holds true for spelling; if you don't read carefully, you may swear a particular word is spelled correctly when it's actually wrong. Double-check anything you are not 100 percent positive is right.

If you've included quotations and paraphrases from outside sources, you should also double-check the citations. Make certain you've given each source credit and followed the right format.

Turning in an essay that is not carefully edited makes a very poor impression on a teacher. It indicates that you don't take your work all that seriously. Even if the ideas within the essay are good, not taking the time to edit can lower your grade significantly. Make certain you take the time to edit and that you do it carefully.

After you've completed editing the essay, type up or print out the final version. Most teachers require that an essay be typed. However, even if it is not required, all college-level essays, and most high-school-level ones, should be typed. Handwritten essays are difficult for a teacher to read and do not appear as professional as typed ones. By typing an essay, you indicate you take your work seriously.

A Proofreader's Guide

Always proofread your essay after you have finished revising it and before turning it in. When you proofread, you are looking for errors specifically in grammar, spelling, and punctuation. However, it can often be difficult to catch them because, being accustomed to the essay as it stands, you simply do not see them. In order to proofread effectively, you need to read in a much more focused manner.

When you are ready, try to use a clean copy of the essay. This is easy if you are working on a computer, as you can simply print one out. Find a location to read in where there are absolutely no distractions. It is extremely important that the entire time you read, you keep foremost in your mind that you are trying to locate errors. If you forget this and get caught up in the content of the essay, you will continue to overlook mistakes. Read slowly and methodically, concentrating on each word and sentence. It is extremely helpful to read out loud, so that you can hear each word; you can also simply mouth the words silently.

Some people recommend reading the essay backward. By reading backward, you are not distracted by the writing itself and instead focus on individual words. While this is an effective way to spot spelling errors, it does not enable you to identify grammar and punctuation errors. You may consider doing both—a "normal" reading and a "backward" one.

By the way, if you are working on a computer, don't depend on the spell-check to catch all the mistakes. The spell-check program is indeed helpful and can correct many errors. However, it doesn't catch everything. For one thing, the spell-check will not catch homophones—words that sound the same but are spelled differently and have different meanings. You should always proofread yourself at least once after you've spell-checked your essay.

Sit with a dictionary in hand while proofreading. Get in the habit of looking up the definition of words you don't use frequently in conversation. In the process of writing and attempting to sound sophisticated, it is easy to use a word you think means one thing when it actually means something quite different.

Additionally, become aware of particular spelling or grammatical errors you are prone to make; whenever you get an essay back from a teacher, read it over to identify them. When you proofread, make certain you look specifically for those mistakes you tend to make.

Proofreading is a tedious process, but it is an important one. Remember, your writing is a reflection of you. A carefully proofread paper indicates a professional and serious attitude. And when the reader is your teacher, isn't that the impression you want to make?

A Proofreading Checklist

Be certain you check the following elements in your final proofreading session. Remember to be on the lookout for those mistakes you tend to make often.

- Spelling errors

- Mixed-up homophones

- Incorrect word usage

- Sentence fragments

- Run-on sentences

- Citation format

- Ambiguous references and pronouns (especially it, that, this, these, and those)

- Pronoun-antecedent agreement

- Comma usage

- Quotation marks (make certain all quotations have quotation marks at the start and end of the quoted section)

- Apostrophes used correctly (especially with possessive nouns and contractions)

- Capitalization

- Consistent verb tense

Read the final version to make certain it is clean, neat, and correct. This is proofreading—the final stage. Correct any typos or other imperfections, and print it out again, if necessary. Include your name and the page number on each page, and staple the pages together. Either on the first page or on a title page, you should also include your name, the professor's name, the name of the course, and of course the title of your essay. The title should make the essay's topic very clear to the reader. You can, though, be a bit creative with the title to make the topic sound interesting and provocative.

It's a good idea to make a copy of the essay before you hand it in to the teacher. More than one teacher has been known to misplace a student's essay.

Computers to the Rescue

Since revision is such a vital component of writing a strong essay, it is highly recommended that you get in the habit of working on a computer. A computer makes it easy to make changes as you revise an essay. You don't necessarily need to own a computer to use one. Most schools now have computer centers where you can sign up for a time to work. Most of them also offer classes and seminars on different computer programs so that you can learn how to use them. If you don't know how to use a computer, this is the time to learn and get in the habit of using it for writing essays.

GIVING CREDIT

Whenever one writer uses another writer's ideas or words and does not give the original writer credit, it is considered plagiarism. Plagiarism is like stealing. Committing plagiarism is a breach of ethics that can have serious repercussions for a student, including a failing grade or being expelled.

The most blatant form of plagiarism is copying an entire essay from another student or source. It is also plagiarism if you include information from another source within your essay and don't credit the source. Even one uncredited sentence or phrase can be considered plagiarism. You probably won't be expelled over one or two uncredited sentences, but failing to document sources can lower your grade.

When you are assigned an essay that requires research, you are obviously allowed to consult sources. You just need to be very careful that you always give credit to these sources whenever you use them.

As you might imagine, quoting from, paraphrasing, and crediting sources can become quite messy, especially if you aren't consistent about the way you do it. To help make essays readable, standard formats have been developed to provide consistency within an essay and from one essay to another. Ask your professor which format to use and make certain you follow it. The most popular currently used in most schools are those developed by the Modern Language Association (MLA) and American Psychological Association (APA), and known as the MLA and APA formats. You can purchase a handbook for either one.

In general, these standard formats consist of two components: citations within the essay and the list of works cited at the essay's conclusion. Whenever you quote or paraphrase a source, you include a citation with the sentence or passage that indicates which source it comes from, as well as the page number within the source. These citations are usually abbreviations for the whole source, such as the author's last name or a key word in the source's title. The citation corresponds to a listing in the Works Cited section, at the end of the essay, where the full publication information for each source is listed. There are specific formats for listing sources, and for different types of sources, in the Works Cited section. Your professor will specify a specific format, and you can purchase a handbook to help you with it.

Remember, always give credit where credit is due.

Sample Essay Paragraph with Citations from Other Sources (MLA Format)

The repetitions of various images and themes in <u>Long Day's Journey into Night</u> enables O'Neill to reveal past information without resorting to unrealistic methods. In the smaller groupings, characters discuss their past lives a great deal, but it does not seem unnatural or forced because O'Neill takes great pains to tell us that these arguments about the past often take place (Tiusanen 117, Chothia 169-170). As Laurin Porter explains, characters in the play anticipate each other's lines and arguments, an indication of how often these discussions take place (87). For example, Jamie tells Tyrone he "could see that line coming! God, how many thousand times!" (33). Characters often acknowledge the repetitious nature of their arguing, such as when Jamie tells Mary that he and Tyrone have been arguing over "the same old stuff" (40) and when Mary tells the boys, "you've heard me say this a thousand times" (61). O'Neill thereby does more than merely tell us that the family fights about the past constantly; he actually shows them doing it, emphasizing how much the past still dominates the present for them.

Works Cited
(This would appear at the end of the essay that contains the above paragraph; each reference to an outside source in the text corresponds to a listing in the Works Cited.)

Chothia, Jean. <u>Forging a Language: A Study of the Plays of Eugene O'Neill.</u> Cambridge: Cambridge University Press, 1979.

O'Neill, Eugene. <u>Long Day's Journey into Night.</u> New Haven: Yale University Press, 1955.

Porter, Laurin. <u>The Banished Prince: Time, Memory and Ritual in the Late Plays of Eugene O'Neill.</u> Ann Arbor: UMI Research Press, 1988.

Tiusanen, Timo. "Through the Fog into the Monologue: Long Day's Journey into Night." in <u>Eugene O'Neill: A Collection of Criticism.</u> Ed. Ernest G. Griffin. New York: McGraw-Hill, 1976. 114-129.

COMMON GRAMMATICAL ERRORS

Your ideas are the most vital part of any essay; without strong ideas, an essay will not be impressive, no matter how well written it is. However, correct grammar is also important; correct grammar makes it easier for the reader to understand and appreciate your ideas in the first place.

There are many different grammar rules. You can't possibly memorize them all, but you don't necessarily have to. You learn to speak without learning the "rules" of conversation by listening to others; you can also learn about grammar and language usage by reading. The more you read, the more you develop an "ear" for correct grammar. When you write, something will "sound" right or wrong to you. Try to read more frequently and trust your "ear" for correct grammar. However, if you have a serious problem with grammar, you may consider working with a tutor.

Here is a list of some of the more common errors in grammar, punctuation, and language usage. These are errors you should particularly watch out for when you are proofreading your essay.

• HOMOPHONES

Homophones are words that sound alike but have different spellings and meanings; they are extremely easy to confuse in your writing. Even when you proofread carefully, they can escape your attention and a computer's spell-checker cannot distinguish between them. Watch out for homophones and make certain you have chosen the correct word.

These are some of the most commonly confused homophones:

    its/it's
    your/you're
    two/too/to
    there/their/they're
    whose/who's

• SENTENCE FRAGMENTS

A sentence fragment is a group of words that does not function as a complete sentence. A complete sentence must consist of an independent clause—a group of words that includes a subject and verb and

Spell Well

Here's a list of frequently misspelled, commonly used words; in fact, they're probably words you misspell every time you use them without even realizing it. Most often these are misspelled because people get one or two letters wrong. Make certain you are familiar with these words so you can watch for them in your writing and double-check to see if they are correct.

absence	independent	seize
accessible	indispensable	self/selves
accommodate	insistent	separate
acquaintance	interpret	significance
achieve	judgment	sophomore
across	(or judgement)	succeed/successful
appearance	knowledge	terrific
athlete	loneliness	their
bureaucracy	medicine	tragedy
business	noticeable	transfer/transferred
changeable	occasionally	undoubtedly
commitment	occur/occurred/	unnecessary
committed	occurrence	vacuum
conscience	omit/omitted	worshipped
definitely	parallel	
difference/different	peace/peaceable	
embarrass	perseverance	
emphasize	preference/preferred	
exaggerate	prevalence	
exercise	privilege	
existence	pursue	
exorcise	refer/referred	
guarantee	referring	
half/halves	repetition	
indefinitely	rhythm	

can stand on its own. The most common type of sentence fragments are those that lack either subjects or verbs. You can usually correct a fragment by adding a subject or verb, or by joining together separate fragments and not forgetting to add a comma.

Fragments:
Ate dinner at home. (no subject)
His next-door neighbor the doctor. (no verb)

Complete Sentences:
Mark ate dinner at home.
His next-door neighbor is a doctor.

When you proofread your essay, make certain each sentence has both a subject and a verb.

RUN-ON SENTENCES

Run-on sentences are the opposites of fragments. While a fragment does not contain an independent clause, a run-on sentence strings one clause or phrase after another, confusing the reader.

Example:

A Doll's House is a play by Henrik Ibsen that depicts a middle-class marriage where the husband treats the wife, Nora, like a doll but in the end she asserts her independence and she decides to leave him but first she sits him down and tells him the reasons why she is leaving and says she realizes she had been living an illusion with him and had never really done what she wanted.

As you can see in the above sentence, a run-on is very confusing to read; you get lost somewhere in the middle of the sentence and forget what the whole thing is about. Most run-on sentences can be rewritten as two or three shorter sentences.

A Doll's House is a play by Henrik Ibsen that depicts a middle-class marriage. The husband treats the wife, Nora, like a doll. In the end, she asserts her independence and decides to leave him. First she sits him down and tells him the reasons why she is leaving. She says she realizes she has been living an illusion and has never really done what she wanted.

PRONOUN-ANTECEDENT AGREEMENT

Pronouns (he, she, him, her, his, hers, their, theirs, it, its) take the place of nouns, and the nouns they refer to are

Dazed and Confused

The following list contains words or expressions that are frequently confused or misused. Most of them are homophones, words that sound the same but are spelled differently and have different meanings. Get to know the words on this list so you can watch out for them in your writing and double-check to make certain you use them correctly.

principle/principal
> **principle.** A rule or law; a fact of nature.
> **principal.** A person in authority, such as the head of a school. (Remember, the principal is your pal.)

capital/capitol
> **capital.** The seat of government (such as the city that is the state capital).
> **capitol.** The building in which a governing body meets (as in the Capitol in Washington, D.C.).

affect/effect
> **affect.** Used as a verb meaning to influence or to change.
> *The noise* affects *my ability to think.*
> **effect.** Used as a noun, meaning the result of something.
> The noise produces a negative effect on my work.

stationary/stationery
> **stationary.** Standing still.
> **stationery.** Materials used for writing and typing.
> *The clerk was* stationary *behind the stationery counter.*

than/then
> **than.** Used when comparing.
> **then.** Used in reference to time; the next in order or time.
> *I'd rather eat lunch and* then *go to the movies, rather* than *the other way around.*

Dazed and Confused *(cont.)*

your/you're
your. A possessive; refers to something you own.
you're. A contraction of "you are."
You're *going to be late to pick up* your *car.*

their/there
their. A possessive; refers to something they own.
there. Refers to location.
Their *car is over* there *in that parking lot.*

its/it's
its. A possessive; refers to what "it" owns.
it's. A contraction of "it is."
It's *fun to watch the dog fetch* its *toys.*

center on/revolve around
It is incorrect to say that something centers *around* or revolves on a subject; something can only center on or revolve *around* a subject.

quote/quotation
quote. Used as a verb meaning to repeat something from another source.
quotation. Used as a noun meaning the reference that is repeated from another source.
He proceeded to quote *from the passage, and the* quotation *was quite long.*

media/medium
medium. A singular form of the word media referring to a single type of mass communication such as radio or television.
media. A plural form of the word medium that refers to several types of communication or to mass communication in general.
Television is a medium *that is far more influential and important than the other* media.

called antecedents. Pronouns and antecedents must always agree, which means they must both be either singular or plural.

Example:

Incorrect (Pronoun and Antecedent Do Not Agree)
The students took his tests.

Correct (Pronoun and Antecedent Are Both Plural)
The students took their tests.

There are two cases where this grammatical issue particularly becomes a problem: indefinite pronouns and generic nouns. An indefinite pronoun refers to a nonspecific person or thing, such as anybody, anyone, everybody, or someone. A generic noun represents a typical member of a group, such as a doctor, a student, or a New Yorker. Both of these antecedents are followed by *singular* pronouns: You should either use "he," "she," or "one" as the pronoun, or rewrite the sentence to avoid the problem.

Incorrect:
When everyone has finished their exam, the test is over.
A doctor must be considerate of their patients' feelings.

Correct:
When everyone has finished his or her exam, the test is over.
A doctor must be considerate of his or her patients' feelings.

• AMBIGUOUS REFERENCES

Broad, non-specific references, such as this, that, which, and it, are ambiguous; it's not always clear what they refer to, which can confuse your reader. You should clearly indicate the person, object, subject, or idea these words refer to.

Ambiguous Phrasing:
Hamlet screams at Ophelia and tells her to go to a

nunnery. This eventually drives her insane.

More Clearly Phrased As:
Hamlet screams at Ophelia and tells her to go to a nunnery. This treatment of her eventually drives her insane.

Similarly, when you use pronouns such as he, she, him, her, his, or hers, make certain the reader knows the specific person to whom the pronoun refers.

Ambiguous Phrasing:
Claudius and Hamlet fight. He kills him.

In the example above, we don't know who kills and who is killed. Those sentences can be more clearly phrased:
Claudius and Hamlet fight. Hamlet kills the king.

• DANGLING MODIFIERS

Modifiers are words or phrases that describe or elaborate upon some other word or phrase. Dangling modifiers do not logically refer to any word in the sentence and therefore make the sentence incoherent. Be particularly careful when a sentence begins with a modifier; whatever subject follows the

modifier must be the one the modifier refers to:

Incorrect:
Originally performed in 1955, many people still consider *Cat on a Hot Tin Roof* to be Tennessee Williams's greatest play.

In the above sentence, the modifier "originally performed in 1955" refers to the play *Cat on a Hot Tin Roof*, and not the "many people." The sentence should therefore be rephrased:

Correct:
Originally performed in 1955, *Cat on a Hot Tin Roof* is still considered by many people to be Tennessee Williams's greatest play.

• SPLIT INFINITIVES

An infinitive form of a verb consists of two parts: the word "to" plus the verb. An infinitive is "split" when another word, usually an adverb, comes between them. Although certain constructions featuring split infinitives have come to be accepted, they generally sound awkward and disrupt the flow of a sentence. You should generally avoid them.

Split Infinitive:

My parents taught me to slowly eat.

Intact Infinitive:

My parents taught me to eat slowly.

• SENTENCES ENDING IN PREPOSITIONS

Prepositions are certain words, usually appearing at the beginning of a phrase, that are used to describe or elaborate on some other word in the sentence.

There are a limited number of prepositions in English. The most common include: about, above, across, after, against, along, among, around, as, at, before, behind, below, beside, between, but, by, concerning, despite, during, except, for, from, in, into, like, near, next, of, off, on, onto, out, over, regarding, respecting, since, than, through, throughout, to, toward, under, underneath, unlike, until, unto, up, upon, with, without.

It is generally considered poor grammar to end a sentence with a preposition. If a sentence ends with a preposition, you should rephrase it.

Incorrect:

He couldn't get around the couple so he walked between. She didn't understand what the remark referred to.

Correct:

He couldn't get around the couple so he walked between them. She didn't understand to what the remark referred.

Say it with Style

Every piece of writing has its own distinctive style. The style reflects the manner something is written in, and depends on such factors as the choice of words, the sentence patterns, and the way ideas are introduced. An essay's style indicates the writer's attitude toward the material, and signals to the reader how to respond. For example, the style can indicate if a work is serious, sarcastic, humorous, or silly.

When you are writing an academic essay, you generally want to use a serious, intelligent style. Avoid being too chatty or conversational. You don't want to use slang or casual expressions; instead, you should use a sophisticated vocabulary. You also want to write sentences that are more varied and complex in structure than "See Dick run." At the same time, you don't want to overdo it. If you try too hard to write in an academic manner, you might make the essay too stilted or confusing.

Consider the following examples.

Too Conversational:
Long Day's Journey into Night is such a bummer to read. The Tyrone family is really, really having a lousy time trying to communicate. They should like, really get with it and start dealing with like, stuff.

Too Wordy and Overwritten:
Eugene O'Neill's magnum opus, *Long Day's Journey into Night*, bears upon the reader with the weight of its tragic philosophizing on the historicity of this particular familial unit. The Tyrones, as they are deemed in the work, are prey to such overpowering dramatic forces, such as fate, the gods, their genes, and the distinctive, saturnine environmental setting, which is incidentally an obvious homage to

the great naturalist works of Zola and Strindberg. These four lost souls need to penetrate the steel-like veneer of familial normalcy and at last examine their flaws, failings, and feelings.

Sophisticated Yet Direct Style: *Long Day's Journey into Night* undoubtedly has a powerful effect upon any contemporary reader. The Tyrones are clearly a dysfunctional family grappling, like so many families, with issues of communication. One senses that if the family would cease dredging up past events, they could at last address their present problems and make positive changes for the future.

The last paragraph makes an intelligent comment about the play and weaves in some sophisticated vocabulary. However, it remains a direct, easy-to-read statement that will not confuse the reader and will impress a teacher.

Write with style, but make certain it is a style appropriate for an essay. Let your writing indicate intelligence and sophistication, without being too highbrow or convoluted.

A WORD ON WORDS

If you read an essay that uses the same words over and over, it can become quite boring and tedious. To make your writing more interesting for your reader, try to vary your choice of words as much as possible. You particularly want to use a sophisticated vocabulary that reflects your intelligence and expertise.

To help increase word variety, you can use a thesaurus—a special dictionary of synonyms. (Synonyms are words that have similar meanings.) You can buy a thesaurus in most bookstores. Try to find one that is organized like a dictionary, with words listed in alphabetical order and their possible synonyms beneath them.

When you edit your paper, look for any words that are repeated, especially within the same paragraph. Use the thesaurus to select alternatives.

For example, the following passage repeats variations on the same word:

Long Day's Journey into Night illustrates the many tensions in the Tyrone family. The family members' relationships are fraught with tension. Each conversation between family members is also tense.

With the help of a thesaurus, you can easily find synonyms that make the passage more varied and interesting:

Long Day's Journey into Night illustrates the many tensions in the Tyrone family. The family members' relationships are fraught with strain and anxiety. Each conversation between family members is uneasy.

When using a thesaurus, you do need to be careful about which synonym you choose. Although synonyms have similar meanings, there are subtle differences that are important. Certain words are also more appropriate for a particular context. Additionally, some of the synonyms in the thesaurus might be old-fashioned words not frequently used. If you include them in your essay, these words will stand out and disrupt the flow of your argument. You should therefore only choose synonyms you are familiar with and comfortable using in your writing. If necessary, you can look up some of the suggested synonyms in a dictionary in order to see the exact definition and appropriate context.

Variety Is the Spice of Writing: Using a Thesaurus

When you use the same word or similar forms of a word too often, an essay is repetitive and tedious to read. By varying word choice, you can make the essay much more interesting.

The thesaurus is a vital resource for word choices. A thesaurus is simply a reference book that lists synonyms for particular words. Synonyms are words that share the same meaning. A thesaurus also might include antonyms, which are words that have the opposite meanings.

There are several types of thesauruses on the market, and some are easier to use than others. Look for one that is organized in dictionary form, listing words in alphabetical order followed by their many synonyms and antonyms. Using this kind is easy. With a thesaurus that is not organized in dictionary form, you'll find instead cross listings and cross-references and have a harder time. When you look for a particular word, you won't necessarily find synonyms for it; instead, you'll be referred to another word or part of a word, where you then find a more extensive listing of synonyms.

Have the thesaurus handy as you edit your essay. Look for any word repetitions, especially if they appear in the same sentence or paragraph. Then, look up that word in the thesaurus and choose an alternative word from the list of synonyms.

You do need to be careful when using the thesaurus, however. Many of the synonyms may not be appropriate for your essay. Synonyms share similar meanings, but are seldom identical. Certain synonyms might only be appropriate for certain topics or issues, or they might be old-fashioned or outdated and no longer used in most writing. You should only choose a synonym you are familiar with and comfortable using. You might also want to look up the definition of the synonym in a dictionary to ensure that the meaning of the word fits your sentence.

PUT YOUR BEST FOOT FORWARD

Your writing is one of the most direct forms of communication between you and your teacher. What your teacher sees in your writing contributes significantly to the impression he or she has of you. An essay that is sloppy and unfocused, filled with typos and grammatical errors, pains a portrait of a student who doesn't care all that much about what he or she has turned in. However, an essay that is neat, well-organized, filled with interesting and original ideas, and carefully proofread indicates the student takes pride in his or her work. You can guess which student will get a higher grade on the essay—and for class participation. Remember, your essay tells the teacher a lot more than your ideas about a particular subject.

Important Points to Remember

1. Writing is communication.

2. The quality of your ideas is the most important element of your writing.

3. Your writing reflects you; make certain your essay shows you have a serious, professional attitude toward your work.

4. Learn to use the library to your advantage.

5. Write in stages: think, research, organize, draft, revise, edit, and proofread. Each time you revise, you make the essay a little better.

6. Be organized. Create a strategic plan of action and follow it.

7. Be the guide for your reader through the essay; make certain your reader can follow one idea to the next and won't have major questions about your main points.

8. When proofreading, be on the lookout for trouble spots, especially the mistakes you tend to make often.

CHAPTER 5

Taking Tests

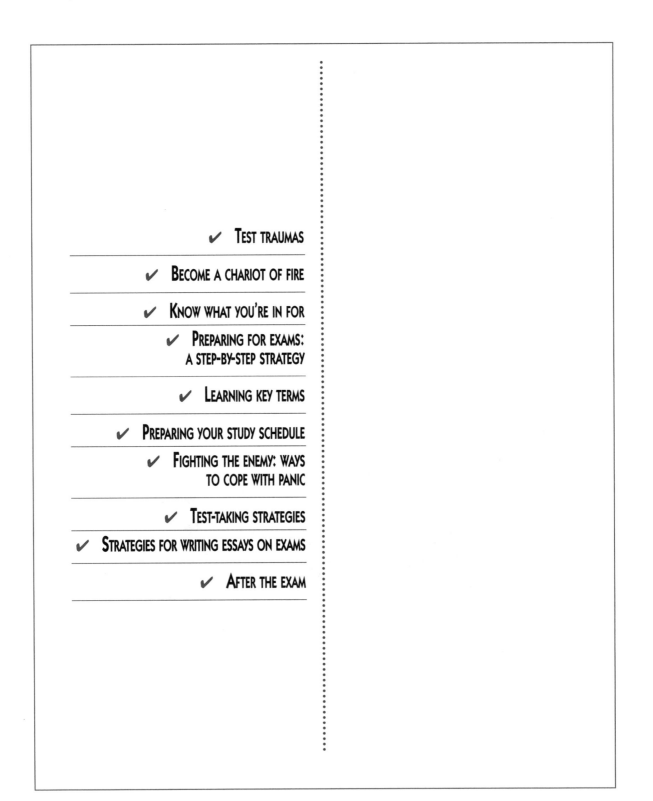

The Mad Crammer

Although the Mad Crammer tries to make it to most of his classes, he doesn't bother doing any work outside of class, like the required reading assignments. He figures there'll be plenty of time for that later in the semester. But before he knows it, finals week has arrived and he's got only two days to prepare for four exams. Drinking coffee by the gallon, he stays awake night and day poring over his books, forcing himself to remember as much as he can. He shows up at his first exam bleary-eyed, with a killer headache. When the exam is passed out, he can barely read the questions, let alone answer them. Much of the material on the exam looks vaguely familiar, but when he tries to remember more exact information, he finds everything muddled in his mind. When he gets to the essay section, he's relieved to see the question relates to material he had read the night before. He begins writing but, after a few paragraphs, he is completely

exhausted and just doesn't have the energy to continue.

The Mid-Exam Panicker

Unlike the Crammer, the Mid-Exam Panicker methodically prepares for an upcoming exam. She begins studying two weeks before finals and goes into the exam confident she'll ace it. She breezes through the first section, all multiple choice questions. But when she comes to the first essay, she is horrified to find that she doesn't understand the question at all. She starts to feel

sick to her stomach and her pulse begins to race. Figuring she'll come back to the question later, she goes on to the next essay question. She begins to write, but all she can think about is the question she skipped. How many points was it worth? Will she fail the exam? Will she fail the course? Will she have to drop out of school? Will she ever get a job if they hear about how she did on this exam? Unable to write, she keeps thinking about that one question, right until the proctor announces that time is up.

The Alarmist

Whenever the Alarmist sees someone from his class, he corners him or her and launches into his typical speech: "I heard that Professor Abrams's exams are just impossible. Last year like thirty people failed the exam. I don't see how I'm going to pass. How are you going to pass? What have you studied? Have you studied chapter 12? I heard chapter 12 is the one Abrams always asks questions on. Oh, and you better study all the charts in the appendix, because he asked about that last year. And I heard that this year's exam is going to be the hardest ever." When the exams are returned, the Alarmist is surprised to find he did quite well. Three of the people he had spoken to before the exam, though, failed. They had spent the entire night studying chapter 12, which was never on the exam.

BECOME A CHARIOT OF FIRE

If you've been following the strategies outlined in earlier chapters for taking notes on lectures and reading assignments, then, believe it or not, you've already completed the bulk of your studying. By following those strategies, you've been working with and thinking about concepts relevant to the course all semester; you've gained a comfortable familiarity with the subject and have made it an integrated part of your general knowledge. You could probably go into an exam right now and pass it. However, as the Test Traumas above demonstrate, if you don't prepare for an examination the right way or have the wrong attitude, you are in for some trouble.

You may think that passing an examination is solely a matter of how much of the course material you've got memorized. As the above examples demonstrate, an exam is just as much a test of mental and physical endurance as it is your knowledge of a particular subject. In that sense, it's somewhat akin to running a marathon. Even though most marathon runners run every day, they

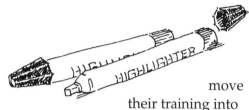

move their training into high gear during the weeks before a major race, running longer hours and further distances so they will be ready for the upcoming event.

You, too, should move your studying into high gear before a test, focusing your energy more on the subject matter. The methods and strategies outlined here will help you do that. You probably won't be surprised to find that, as with the strategies earlier in the book, the key here is to make the study process active. Many students think studying means reading their notes over and over again. There's no guarantee, though, that the more times you read something, the better you'll answer questions on it. You don't need to be a bookworm or genius to ace a test, but you do need to be a "chariot of fire," willing to train hard with the goal of capturing a winning grade on an upcoming exam.

KNOW WHAT YOU'RE IN FOR

One of the things that causes panic in any situation is fear of the unknown. If you don't know what's lurking behind a door, you might very well be afraid to open it, especially when your imagination goes to work and transforms whatever is behind that door into a ax-wielding maniac. Your imagination can also convince you that an upcoming exam will include killer-questions impossible to answer. You can put your mind at ease, though, by finding out as much as possible about an exam *before* you go into the examination room.

In addition to alleviating panic, knowing something about the format of an exam can help you plan your study schedule more efficiently. There are different ways to study for different types of examination questions. If you have an idea of the kinds of questions likely to be asked, you can tailor your study schedule to prepare specifically for those questions.

Here are some ways to find out about an upcoming exam:

1. Talk to the Professor

The most obvious source for information about an exam is the professor; after all, the professor is the one who makes up the questions. Most professors will take a few minutes during a class to explain the format and the material to be covered. If an exam is approaching and the professor has not made such an announcement, you can take the initiative and ask.

Although you can ask in class, talking to the professor after class or during office hours is, in some ways, more effective. The professor will be more inclined to talk with you at length when it's not taking up other students' time. You'll therefore be able to ask more questions and, if you're lucky, the professor might offer you more detailed information about the exam than he did in class.

These are some basic questions you can ask a professor about an upcoming exam:

- What will be the format of the exam? Will there be short answer questions? What type?

Multiple choice questions? Will there be essays? A combination of types of questions?

- How many sections will there be on the exam? How many points will each section be worth?
- How much of your overall grade does the exam count for?
- What material from class will be covered on the exam?
- If the exam is a final, will the exam be cumulative (meaning it covers the entire semester's worth of material)? Or will it only cover a portion of the course material?
- Does the professor have any suggestions on how to study for the exam?

Try to see the professor at least one week before a scheduled exam; that gives you enough time to plan your study schedule accordingly. However, there's no reason why you can't ask about an exam much earlier in the semester. While the professor may not have made up the exam yet, she probably has an idea of what the overall format will be and the material it will cover. If you get this information, you can keep it in mind and be on the lookout for possible exam questions as you take notes from classroom lectures and readings.

2. Try to Find Exams on the Same (or Similar) Courses

You can get a highly accurate sense of what an upcoming exam will be like by looking at previous exams. In addition to providing examples of the kinds of questions likely to be included, these can be used for practice runs to test yourself on the course material.

Some departments keep exams on file so that students may use them as a study resource. You can also try to find someone who has already taken the course and held onto the exams, and who is willing to lend them to you. Just make certain that you are not doing anything unethical in looking at old examinations. If the professor has given a graded exam back to the students, then she knows it is available for anyone to examine. However, if the professor collects the exams and does not return them, then she doesn't intend for them to be distributed among students. If you somehow get a pirated copy of an exam, you are committing a serious breach of ethics that can get you in big trouble. When you consider the penalties, you'll realize that it's just not worth the risk; there are plenty of other study resources you can use.

Ideally you want to find an old exam for the same course you are taking that was made up by your professor. This provides you with the most accurate picture of the exam you can expect to take. If you can't find an old exam written by your professor, you can try to track down exams for the same course given by other professors. Although these exams might not include the exact questions your teacher will ask, they provide a general sense of the questions frequently asked. It is also easier to find old exams when you don't limit your search to your own professor. For example, you can borrow exams from friends at other schools who have taken the same course.

You can also learn a great deal by looking at exams your own professor has given for *other* courses. While you may not get any clues about the exact questions likely to appear on your upcoming exam, you will get a sense for the kinds of questions your professor asks and their overall level of difficulty.

3. Listen for Clues

Throughout the semester, keep your ears open for any clues about what might be on an exam. Clues can crop up anytime, so be on the lookout. A professor might say, in a completely casual manner, that a particular concept or term is likely to show up on the exam. After making a certain point, a teacher might say something like, "If I were to ask a question on an exam about this topic, I'd ask you . . ." Anytime your professor makes any reference to an exam, even in an offhand manner, make certain you note and star it.

In addition to blatant clues, the professor will probably give you subtle ones. Exam questions always reflect the professor's personal interests and biases. Even if the course is a basic survey course, there are certain to be some topics your teacher feels are more important for you to know and are therefore more likely to show up on an exam. Anything your professor seems particularly serious or passionate about is a likely candidate for inclusion. Any point your professor makes repeatedly, or gives special attention to, is also more likely to appear on an exam. Star these points in your notes to remind yourself to study them before an exam.

PREPARING FOR EXAMS: A STEP-BY-STEP STRATEGY

1. Read over all notes from class lectures and reading assignments.

2. Create master lists from notes.

3. Work with the master lists and quiz yourself.

4. Get help from other sources.

1. Read Over All Notes from Class Lectures and Reading Assignments

Many students begin to panic before an exam because they've left themselves way too much to worry about at the last minute; an examination approaches, and they find they still have to read assignments they never got to, reread assignments they don't remember, scrounge up notes for lectures they missed, and figure out what their own notes mean if they've forgotten.

However, if you have been following the methods outlined in earlier chapters, you should already have clear, comprehensive notes from classroom lectures and reading assignments that include just about everything you need to know for an exam.

To begin studying for an upcoming exam, gather together all your notes from the course in one binder. This should not be a problem, since you've been putting your notes in a binder at home throughout the semester. Just make certain you now have them all in one place, in a logical order.

The first step is to read these notes from start to finish. It is extremely important that you do this in one sitting, *without interruption*. This will help you concentrate more intently on the material; more importantly, it will enable you to develop a clear picture in your mind of the course material as a whole. Rather than studying various bits and pieces of information related to the subject, you'll now be able to see how everything fits together as part of the overall course.

For each examination, set aside several hours to read through your notes from beginning to end. However, don't study several subjects at once or one subject right after another. If you study several courses within a short period of time, the material can easily become mixed up in your mind, making it more difficult for you to remember specific details. Make certain you take a break of at least two hours before sitting down to read notes from another course.

2. *Create Master Lists from Notes*

As you read over your notes, condense and reorganize the material onto three single sheets of paper—the three master lists. The preparation of these lists is itself a part of the study process; by reorganizing the material, you gain a firmer grasp on the course. At the same time, the master lists serve as study tools; rather than having to read through all your notes again, you only need to study these three sheets. Each master list prepares you for a specific kind of examination question.

THE MASTER LIST OF KEY TERMS

Create a master list of key terms from your notes by writing down any names, dates, concepts, or ideas that are central to the course; do not add any definition or explanation of them. Try to squeeze all the key terms on a single sheet of paper. Don't write down any of them more than once; even if one comes up repeatedly throughout the course, you only need to write it down once. You may also decide to eliminate some key terms from the master list because you realize, in retrospect, that they aren't all that important.

THE MASTER LIST OF GENERAL THEMES

Create a master list of general themes. As with the master list of key terms, try to squeeze all the general themes onto a single sheet of paper. If a particular theme recurs throughout the course, you don't need to write it down more than once; however, you should put a star beside it to indicate its importance.

THE MASTER LIST OF RELATED CONCEPTS

Creating this particular master list is a bit more complicated and will likely take more thought and effort than the other two. However, it will prove helpful in preparing for examination questions of all kinds.

As you read through your notes, try to identify groups of concepts that relate closely to one another. If you've identified such a group, write it down on the master list of related concepts and give it a subject heading.

A common category of related concepts is a principle or idea and the various examples that illustrate or support it. For example, you might be taking a history course in which the professor has argued repeatedly that the latter half of the Middle Ages was marked by an increased pessimism and despair. You might then group together the various events your professor described that indicate this trend.

Reasons for Increased Pessimism in the Fourteenth and Fifteenth Centuries

- Weak kings (Edward II, Richard II) whose power was threatened by the barons
- One Hundred Years' War
- The Black Plague (1348)
- Skepticism in the church (after sale of pardons is sanctioned)

Here are other ways to group related concepts together that you might include on your master list:

- Events and causes (that lead up to them)
- Rules and exceptions
- Similar ideas, concepts, theories, and examples
- Opposite or dissimilar ideas, concepts, theories, and examples
- Chronologies/datelines
- Causes and effects

Try to identify and write down as many of these groups as you can. However, there are any number of ways to organize ideas and you won't be able to identify each and every one. The process of reorganizing your notes this way encourages you to think, using the same kind of logic behind most examination questions.

You might have trouble, at first, fitting all the groups you identify on a single sheet of paper. If this is the case, use more than one sheet. As you work more with the master list, you can make decisions about what to eliminate and eventually condense the list onto a single sheet.

3. Work with the Master Lists and Quiz Yourself

After your initial reading of all your notes, you should have created three separate master lists—key terms, general themes, and related concepts. The bulk of your preparation for the exam will center on working with these master lists. Each one includes information that will help answer a particular type of question.

WORKING WITH THE LIST OF KEY TERMS

Many short-answer questions, such as multiple choice, fill in the blank and true or false questions, are specifically designed to test your factual knowledge, to see if you know about something of significance or the meaning of a particular term. You

can't figure out the answer to these questions using reasoning or other kinds of skills—either you know the answer or you don't.

All the following sample questions test factual knowledge of key terms.

1. An elegy is:
   A. a poetic inscription that ends with a witty turn of thought
   B. a fourteen-line poem written in iambic pentameter
   C. a formal poetic lament after the death of a particular person
   D. a long narrative poem documenting heroic actions

2. A fourteen-line poem written in iambic pentameter is:
   A. a sonnet
   B. an epigram
   C. an epic
   D. an elegy

3. A _____ is a long narrative poem documenting heroic actions.

While short answer questions might test you on factual knowledge, you'll also need to know these facts to write essays. As we'll soon see, your primary goal in answering an essay question is to demonstrate to the professor your knowledge and mastery of the subject matter. Therefore, the more key terms you weave into an essay answer, the more you will impress the teacher with your knowledge.

For this reason, becoming very familiar with the key terms is a crucial part of preparing for an examination. For some terms, you will need to provide definitions; for others, you will need to know something that is relevant to the course. This is particularly the case with names of people, places, characters, and dates. For example, on a psychology exam, you might need to define the term "id." However, you might also need to know significant facts *about* Freud, such as that he conceived of the model of human personality consisting of the id, ego, and superego.

Therefore, as part of your exam preparation, you should spend a certain amount of time learning and testing yourself on the key terms. After you have completed your master list, quiz yourself on the terms. Go down the list and try to define or say something significant about each term on the list. If possible, quiz yourself in private and discuss each term out loud, as if you were explaining it to someone else in the room. This procedure ensures that you explain each term fully. Many times, you look at a term, think you know it, and skip to the next one. However, you may not really be able to define the term as easily or as clearly as you think. By talking about each term, you see exactly how much you do or don't know about it. You also begin to feel more comfortable discussing these terms at length, which can help when you write an essay response.

LEARNING KEY TERMS

Ultimately, you want to be able to go down the list and confidently define each term or say something about its significance. You probably won't be able to do that on the first shot. You might find yourself unable to remember a certain term or hesitating when you try to define or describe it in detail.

There are then several techniques you can use to learn these key terms. You might, for example, simply go back to your original notes and read more about the term. However, if there are many that give you trouble, this can become a tedious and time-consuming process.

Instead of going back to your original notes, you can create a more detailed master list of key terms that includes brief definitions. Divide this master list into two columns, with the terms in the left column and the definitions in the right. The first few times you quiz yourself on the list, you can look at both columns; seeing the definitions will trigger your memory. After doing this a few times, cover the right column and see how you do when you quiz yourself only looking at the key terms. If you get stuck on a term, simply look at the right column for the definition. Continue quizzing yourself this way until you no longer need to refer to the definitions at all.

TAKE A CUE FROM THE CARDS

The most effective way to memorize key terms is to work with cue cards. Cue cards are particularly helpful when you need to remember a great many key terms, such as new vocabulary words in a foreign language. Simply take 3 x 5 cards and write down a term on one side and either a definition of it or a description of its significance on the other.

Although making the cue cards might seem time consuming, this method has many advantages. First, the process of making the cards helps you begin to memorize the material. As you write down a term and its definition, your mind begins to process the information into your long-term memory. Second, using the cards enables you to shuffle and reorganize them in various ways. For example, you can eliminate cards for terms you know well, and continue to test yourself on the ones you don't.

Third, cue cards enable you to quiz yourself both ways: You can look at the term and test yourself on the definition or look at the definition and try to guess the term. If you can do both, then you truly know the term. This can particularly help on those questions where you need to furnish the term yourself, such as with fill-in-the-blank questions. For this reason, cue cards are also particularly useful in preparing for exams on foreign language vocabulary where you sometimes need to know the English definition of a word and sometimes the foreign word to answer questions.

Cue cards make it very easy for you to test yourself on key terms. Sit with the stack of cards and, for each one, state the definition or description of the term. Then flip the card over to see if you were correct. If you were right and feel pretty confident that you won't forget the term, you can put the card aside. If you got it wrong or had trouble describing it in detail, put the card at the back of the stack. Before you do, though, read over the card a few times and make a concentrated effort to remember it. You won't be able to remember something merely because you've read it; you have to make an effort and instruct yourself to remember it. When you have finished going through the whole stack, shuffle it and start again. Repeat the process, continuing to eliminate any cards you find you know quite well. Eventually you should be able to go through the whole deck and define each term without hesitation. You'll know then that you are ready for the exam.

You won't necessarily be able to go through the whole deck of cue cards successfully in your first sitting. However, that should not concern you. In fact, it's a good idea to work with the cards repeatedly; the more times you practice with the cards, the more likely you'll be able to remember the information on the exam. Try to quiz yourself with the cards several times over the course of several days preceding an exam. One advantage to using cue cards is that you can carry them around with you and quiz yourself anyplace or anytime, even if you are waiting for a bus or during a commercial break while watching television. This will help you make efficient use of your study time before an exam; no free minute has to go to waste.

Even if you use cue cards, you still want to make a master list of key terms on one sheet that you can read over at a glance. As a final test for

yourself before an exam, sit down with a blank sheet of paper and try to write down as many key terms from the course as you can remember. If you can recall almost all of them and what they mean, you are more than ready to take the exam.

IMPROVE YOUR MEMORY

Some people are gifted with photographic memories. They can read a passage of a text and then repeat it word for word from memory. Most people, though, have a great deal of difficulty memorizing information. Like listening, memorizing takes effort. There are, however, a number of strategies to help you improve your memory. These are known as *mnemonic devices*.

Many people think that if they stare at a word, text, or image long enough, they will remember it. By staring at something, they have probably succeeded at inputting the information into their long-term memory. The trouble comes later on, when they try to retrieve that information. Long-term memory is somewhat like a large clothes closet—it can hold an awful lot but, as you put more and more into it, it becomes harder to pick out exactly what you want. Mnemonic devices function as

My Very Elegant Mother...
Mercury, Venus, Earth, Mars...

trigger mechanisms that conjure more detailed information from your long-term memory.

Here are some mnemonic devices and other strategies that can help you memorize information.

RHYMES

Ancient storytellers who didn't know how to read or write could recite epic-length poems completely from memory. They depended on rhythm, alliteration, and especially rhyming words to help trigger their memories of the entire work. For example, if they could remember the first line of a rhymed couplet, the second one would easily come to mind; similarly, if they could remember the rhyming words that ended each couplet, they could usually recall the lines in their entirety.

Throughout history, many people have used short rhymes to help them remember various facts. Some of the more well-known rhymes used for mnemonic purposes are "In 1492, Columbus sailed the ocean blue" and "Thirty days hath September, April, June, and November." You can create your own rhymes to help you remember information about key terms for an exam. Try to find some word that rhymes with the term and write a short phrase or sentence that connects the two together. For example, if you want to remember what a mnemonic device is, you might remember this short rhyme: "Use a mnemonic device so you won't forget twice."

Some terms lend themselves more easily to rhymes than others; if you can't come up with a rhyme relatively quickly, then try some other device so you won't waste much study time.

ALLITERATION

When each word when there are two or more together begins with the same letter or sound, such as "King Kong" or "Peter Piper picked a peck of peppers," you have alliteration. To use alliteration as a mnemonic device, take whatever key term you are trying to memorize and find some word beginning with the same sound that will trigger information about the term.

For example, the word "plethora," according to the dictionary, means "excess" or "abundance." You can associate "plethora" with "plenty." Since both plethora and plenty begin with the letter "P" (in fact, they both begin with the sound "pl"), it's much easier to remember the word "plenty" than "abundance." The word "plenty" makes you think of having too much of something; in other words, an abundance.

MENTAL ASSOCIATIONS

Another way to remember information about a term is to think of a word or image you associate with both the term and its definition. This mental association functions as a link between the term and the information you hope to remember about it.

For example, if you want to remember that Edison created the lightbulb, you can look at Edison's name and see the word "son" in it. "Son" sounds just like "sun," so you can associate Edison's name with the sun. The sun, of course, is a source of light. So, by linking Edison with the sun, you can bring to mind the image of light and the lightbulb.

Similarly, if you wanted to remember that Marconi invented the telegraph, you could stare at Marconi's name and see that it is similar to the word "macaroni." When you think of macaroni, you think of long strings of pasta. When you think of long strings, you think of telegraph wires. Therefore, you can link Marconi to telegraph wires with the image of macaroni.

When you try to create these mental associations, it's often helpful to rely on your personal experiences. For example, one student who needed to remember that John Keats wrote "Ode on a Grecian Urn" thought of her Uncle John who had visited Greece the previous summer. By linking "John" and "Greece" in her mind, she was able to remember that John Keats wrote the poem about the Grecian urn.

You can get as creative as you need to be in finding these associations. If necessary, you can think up a detailed, elaborate story that will help you link a word with information about it. And it can be as silly, illogical, or personal as you like, just so long as it works. A mental association only needs to make sense to you. You don't have to feel obliged to share it with other people.

VISUALIZATIONS

You've probably heard the expression "A picture paints a thousand words." Well, it's also much easier to remember pictures than words. You can therefore use mental images and pictures instead of words and phrases to help you remember something. For example, one way to associate two or more words together is to create a picture in your mind that connects them. If you want to remember that John Keats wrote "Ode on a Grecian Urn," for example, you might picture such an urn filled with enormous keys (which sounds like "Keats") inside of it.

Visualizations can be particularly helpful for associating several different terms or images together. If you want, for example, to remember that the Department of Agriculture is part of the president's Cabinet, you can picture a stalk of corn inside of a large, oak cabinet. You can then add to that image by placing other objects in the cabinet to indicate other departments in the president's Cabinet, such as a giant penny to indicate the treasury, a gun to indicate the defense, and a set of scales to indicate justice.

ACRONYMS

An acronym is a word that is formed by taking the first letters from several words in a series such as SCUBA— S(elf) C(ontained) U(nderwater) B(reathing) A(pparatus). It can be instrumental in helping you remember a long list of items, especially if you need to remember them in a particular order.

For example, to remember the color spectrum, many students memorize the name "Roy G. Biv," an acronym made by taking the first letter of each color in the spectrum in order: R(ed), O(range), Y(ellow), G(reen), B(lue), I(ndigo), V(iolet).

Sometimes the first letters do not make a simple, easy-to-remember name like "Roy G. Biv." In those cases, you can create an entire sentence; the first letter of each word in the sentence corresponds to the first letter of the memorized terms.

For example, in order to remember all of the planets in order, many students memorize this sentence: My very earnest mother just served us nine pickles. The first letter of each word in that sentence corresponds to the first letter of a planet:

My	Mercury
Very	Venus
Elegant	Earth
Mother	Mars
Just	Jupiter
Served	Saturn
Us	Uranus
Nine	Neptune
Pickles	Pluto

Yes, it's a silly sentence. But time and time again, it does the trick. And that's all that matters.

REPEATED EXPOSURE

The more times you expose yourself to material, the more ingrained it becomes in your long-term memory. To make certain you remember something, physically look at and think about it repeatedly over a long period of time. You are much better off studying a list of key terms for an hour each day, for five days, than studying it for five hours on one day.

By looking at the list every day, you train yourself to retrieve that information from your memory after some time has passed. You'll find you get better at remembering information as the week passes; you'll begin to retrieve the information from your memory faster and with less effort.

SLEEP ON IT

In addition to using the above mnemonic devices, there are a few other things you can do to improve your memory. Believe it or not, one thing you can do is sleep. Studies have shown that you are more likely to remember something you've read just before going to sleep. While you are asleep, your mind processes the information, moving it into your long-term memory. There's no guarantee that studying just before bed will be more effective than studying at other times. However, it is certainly worth trying. Try reading over the master list of key terms right before you go to sleep; when you wake up the next morning, quiz yourself and see how much you remember. At the very least, studying the list each night for several nights before an exam ensures you expose yourself to the material repeatedly throughout your study period.

LAST-MINUTE CRAM SHEETS

Sometimes, no matter how hard you study, you will find certain terms extremely difficult to memorize. When all other methods fail, you can create a last-minute cram sheet. The night before an exam, take a single index card and write down any terms, facts, phrases, or formulas you can't remember along with very brief definitions or explanations. Include especially any difficult terms likely to show up on an exam.

Take this card to the exam and arrive at the exam room a few minutes early so you can study the card before the examination begins. (You can sit at a desk in the exam room and study the card if this is allowed; if not, you can find a place to sit outside the room.) Continue to look at the card until you are asked to put away your notes. As soon as you receive your copy of the exam, before you look at a single question, write down everything you remember from the card in the margins of the examination booklet. Since you just looked at the card, the information on it should still be in your short-term memory, which means it should be easy for you to recall. You should be able to remember most of the information for at least five minutes.

The cram card is a particularly effective tool for math and science exams. You can write the formulas on the card and read them over right before the exam. At the start, you can then write the formulas somewhere in the exam book and refer back to them. You won't have to struggle to remember them every time you have to answer a question.

WORKING WITH THE MASTER LIST OF GENERAL THEMES

While preparing for an examination, the list of general themes can give you insight into what to study in detail; test questions almost always relate to the general themes rather than to more obscure points. You can therefore focus primarily on those key terms and concepts that relate to the general themes.

The master list of general themes can also be a valuable tool in preparation for essay examinations. Short-answer questions are fairly limited in scope; each short-answer question focuses on some specific piece of information. An essay question, though, requires elaboration. While answers to short-answer questions are often key terms or phrases, responses to essay questions must be several paragraphs

long. And unlike short-answer questions that provide you with possible answers to choose from, the entire essay comes from a single source—you.

An essay question will therefore be relatively broad. It will not be on some obscure point because there would not be that much to write about. Instead, it will almost always refer to a major aspect of the course. In other words, an essay question almost always

If you bring a cram sheet to the exam, it is very, very important that you put the card away before the exam begins. You are usually free to examine your notes in the minutes before an exam begins. Once the examination officially begins and the proctor instructs you to put your books away, you cannot have any notes out. Don't put it in your pocket or lie it by your desk; instead, put it inside your book bag and put all of your books under your desk. You don't want the card anywhere in sight or you risk being accused of cheating. Even if you weren't actually looking at the card during an exam, a proctor might see it out in the open and assume you were. Don't take that risk. Put the cram card completely out of sight.

reflects one or more of the general themes.

Sometimes an essay question may be a simple reworking of a general theme. For example, if you are taking a course on Shakespeare, a general theme might be: "Shakespeare frequently experimented with the notion of genre; many of his plays defy classification into traditional genres." Possible essay questions that derive from that statement are:

- Discuss how Shakespeare experimented with the concept of genre.
- Choose three Shakespeare plays and discuss how they defy categorization into a specific genre.
- *Romeo and Juliet* is commonly considered an example of Shakespearean tragedy. However, there are a number of elements in it more common to comedy. Write an essay in which you discuss the comic aspects of *Romeo and Juliet*.

The first question essentially restates the general theme from the course into an essay topic. While the other questions are much more specific in terms of what they ask you to discuss, they still relate to the general theme involving the genre of Shakespeare's plays.

When you take an essay examination in class, you are pressed for time. That's why many responses are messy and unorganized. It's hard, after all, to come up with a detailed, focused response right on the spot. However, you've got your master list of general themes, which, as we've just seen, provides you with possible essay questions ahead of time. Examining the list and thinking about each theme, you can plan answers to the essay questions *before* the exam.

You don't, though, have to write an elaborate practice essay for each theme or possible question you come up with. Instead, write down each general theme on a separate piece of paper. For each one, think about how you would approach an essay question related to that theme and make a list of the specific points, topics, and ideas you would incorporate into your response. If there are any key terms that also relate to the theme, list those as well.

Several times before the exam, sit down with these sheets and, using the list of points you've written for each theme, talk your way through the response you will write on the exam. By talking out loud, you will begin to feel more comfortable discussing these themes. Try to do this exercise at least twice for each theme—once looking at the detailed list of points and once looking at only the theme. If you can talk comfortably and at length about a general theme, you can write an essay about it on an exam.

Of course, there's no guarantee that essay questions on the exam will reflect these themes in their original form. However, since most essay questions address broad topics, they will usually connect in some way with a general theme. When you see the essay question, you can identify whichever theme it relates to, and draw on the same concepts you previously thought about in conjunction with that theme as you write.

WORKING WITH THE MASTER LIST OF RELATED CONCEPTS

The answers to many short-answer questions are based on identifying a relationship between different ideas and terms. For example, many multiple choice questions ask you to identify an example of some principle, theory, or idea:

Sample Question:
Which of the following is an example of a simile?
A. "O my love's like a red, red rose"
B. "Death, be not proud, though some have called thee"
C. "Beauty is truth, truth beauty"
D. "Shall I compare thee to a summer's day?"

Sometimes you might have to do the opposite, and identify the larger principle a particular example illustrates:

Sample Question:
"O my love's like a red, red rose" is an example of which type of figurative language?
A. personification
B. metaphor
C. simile
D. hyperbole

These questions can become more complicated when you need to identify several examples of a particular principle or theory and/or eliminate others that don't apply:

Sample Question:
I. "O my love's like a red, red rose"
II. "Higher still and higher/From the earth thou springest/Like a cloud of fire"
III. "Beauty is truth, truth beauty"
IV. "Shall I compare thee to a summer's day?"

Which of the above is/are example(s) of a simile?
A. I and II only
B. III and IV only
C. all of the above
D. none of the above

For all these questions, you need to do more than define the key terms; you need to exercise a sense for which terms go together and why. That's where the master list of related concepts comes in. By having created this list, you've begun thinking with the same logic and in the same terms as the exam questions.

The master list of related concepts is also helpful in preparation for essay questions. In writing an essay, you may need to discuss a particular concept in detail. The master list helps identify the various topics and points that support a particular concept, providing detailed information you can include in your response. Moreover, by looking for the different groups of concepts and identifying how they are related, you have reconceptualized your notes. Being able to rethink and reorganize different concepts indicates you have attained a certain degree of comfort and familiarity with these ideas.

The process of creating this master list involves a great deal of thought and effort. Once you've done it, which is the hard part, all you need to do is read it over a few times before the exam to keep the ideas fresh in your mind. Making this list in advance means you will already have done some serious thinking about the ideas. You can enter an exam feeling confident about your ability to examine, think about, and answer complicated questions.

4. *Get Help from Other Sources*

In the previous chapters on taking notes and reading texts, we saw that you can always turn to other sources for additional information or to get help if you are having trouble. Even if you have begun studying for an exam, it's still not too late to get help.

SEE THE PROFESSOR

Many students become confused or generally anxious when they first sit down to study for a major exam. In need of advice, they turn to the most accessible and most reliable source of information—the professor. However, if you wait to see a professor a few days before an exam and say, "I'm confused. I really need help. What do I do?," it's really too late in the game. However, if you come with a specific question, you can get specific information. On the other hand, if, as you are studying, you come across something that really confuses you, write down a specific question about it. Bring the question to the professor and go over it. In addition to providing you with information, the professor might also offer additional hints about the upcoming exam.

It is also important that you don't rely on the professor as your sole source of help. Once the semester is over, many professors become scarce, which makes it difficult to see them. If you wait to begin studying until after the course has ended, you may not get an opportunity to see the professor. Even if she schedules office hours before an exam, there's no guarantee you'll get to see her—after all, many other students probably have the same idea. Try your best, if you need to, to track down the professor. If you can't, there are other ways to get help.

READING OTHER SOURCES

An important component in the study strategies outlined in previous chapters was reading additional source materials, particularly when you had trouble understanding something from a lecture or reading assignment. If you have enough time, you can still read other sources when you are preparing for an exam. As you go over your notes and prepare the master lists, you may come across terms or ideas that you still don't understand. You also may find that, as time passes, you forget important information. You can turn to other sources or go to the library for more information.

There are many academic encyclopedias and dictionaries, for example, that include listings for the key terms you've studied in class. By consulting these sources, you can find clear and concise explanations of these points. Go to the reference section of the library and ask the librarian to suggest sources.

Even if you are not confused about a particular point, it's a good idea to read some additional sources anyway. The more sources you read about a particular subject, the more information you receive. And by reading about a subject in depth just before an exam, you immerse yourself in the material; you then enter the examination focused on, and comfortable with, that subject.

Consulting introductions to different editions of important primary texts can provide additional information. For example, an introduction to a particular work of literature will often summarize the plot, describe the characters, and discuss major thematic and critical issues. Reading these introductions helps you recall the work in more detail, while providing ideas you might not have considered. You can also look for anthologies and collections that include articles and essays on a particular subject or by a certain writer. For example, an introduction to a volume of *Freud's*

Collected Writings might summarize his major innovations, as well as the controversies surrounding them.

Reading about the same topic in several sources is a worthwhile exercise because it shows how the subject can be described in different ways. This is important as examination questions will often be worded in a manner different from the way the material was originally described to you.

Other sources can also provide a variety of examples and illustrations of

Checklist of Other Sources

- Academic encyclopedias and dictionaries: You can consult general ones such as the Encyclopedia Americana or Encyclopaedia Britannica, or ones for specific subjects, such as arts and humanities, world and U.S. history, or science and technology. Ask the reference librarian for suggestions.
- Introductions to various editions of a particular text, such as a work of literature, or to collections and anthologies of works on specific subjects or by specific writers.
- Additional textbooks on the same subject (remember to check the index and table of contents to find sections you want to read).
- Additional books or articles on the same subject. For suggestions, check:
    —the bibliography or list of works cited in your textbook
    —the subject catalog in the library
    —the section of the library or bookstore where books on that subject are shelved
- Study guides on different subjects specifically written for college students. Just be certain you only use these guides to supplement your own notes, not to take the place of them.

major principles. Finding additional examples can be particularly helpful in preparing for math and science examinations for which you are asked to complete various problems using different formulas. Seeing a variety of sample problems before an exam makes you better prepared to answer problems yourself; you are able to see the many different problems that relate to a particular formula or principle. You can even find sources with sample problems and solutions, so that you can practice with actual questions.

For all these reasons, consulting with and reading additional sources is a valuable study technique in the days prior to an examination. Your priority, however, is creating and working with the three master lists. Only if you have additional time during your study preparation period, should you read other sources.

WORKING WITH STUDY PARTNERS OR STUDY GROUPS

In preparing for an examination, many students decide to work with a partner or to form a study group. This means of studying is not for everyone, however. Before deciding whether or not a study group would help you, consider these advantages and disadvantages:

Advantages:

- When you get together with other students, you have the opportunity to learn from one another. One student, for example, may have better notes or a better grasp of a particular subject than you do. You can use the other students as a source of information to flesh out certain points in your own notes.

- Answering questions from your fellow students will also help you study. Talking about a particular topic is an excellent way to gain familiarity with the material. In the process of describing and explaining a concept to someone else, you come to a better understanding of it yourself.

- Being part of a study group ensures you study a certain amount of time before an exam; the group keeps you on a set study schedule. If you have difficulty motivating yourself to study, being part of a study group can give you the jump start you need.

- Perhaps most importantly, being part of a study group provides emotional support during a difficult time. Studying for and taking exams is an extremely stressful, emotionally draining experience, especially if you feel alone. Meeting regularly with friends going through the same experience can make you feel better. These meetings alleviate tension as you laugh with your friends and help one another through the rough spots.

Disadvantages:

- If the students in your study group have poor notes and don't really understand the subject matter themselves, you might spend all your time helping them and not receive any help in return. You need to watch out for "study moochers" who haven't done any work all year and merely want to copy your notes.

- Panicky students are also a serious problem in a study group. There may be members who are so stressed out that, instead of providing emotional support, they make you more nervous about an exam than you were before. Additionally, the bulk of the study group's time may be spent trying to calm this one person down or

discussing only those concepts he doesn't understand.

- Study groups often don't use time efficiently. You may spend several hours with a study group and find you've only covered a small portion of the material, much less than you could have on your own. There are several reasons why this might occur. Whenever a group of students get together, there is going to be a certain amount of chatting, joking, and socializing taking place. Another problem is that a large portion of time might be spent discussing some point you already understand; that time might be better spent studying something you still don't understand.

Choosing the right people to work with is the way to avoid some of these major disadvantages. A good study group involves give and take among all members; all should be willing to work and should have something valuable to contribute to the group. It's also a good idea to limit the size of the group; any more than five members will probably waste more time and be more trouble than it's worth.

At the same time, if you feel you work better on your own, don't feel you are at a disadvantage. Being in a

study group is no guarantee of study success.

REVIEW SESSIONS

Professors occasionally organize formal review sessions prior to an examination, where they or a teaching assistant are available to answer questions regarding course material. You should attend these study sessions, even if you don't have a question yourself. You never know what hints a professor might give about what will be on the test. It's also helpful to hear the professor or assistant describe again the major concepts and key terms. Try to use some of their phrases and terminology in your essay responses.

Be cautioned, though, that these sessions tend to attract panicky students who use the time to voice their own fears and anxieties about the exam. In addition to wasting time in the session, these students can also make you feel stressed out. Do your best to ignore them. The only person you need to listen to at the review session is the professor or teaching assistant. Another problem, which might arise, is that one or two students will dominate the entire session with their questions. If you have a question, ask it right at the beginning to guarantee you'll be heard.

PREPARING YOUR STUDY SCHEDULE

May

Sun	Mon.	Tues.	Wed.	Thu.	Fri.	Sat.
	1. Study	2. Study	3. Exercise	4. Study	5. Party	6. 1/2 study
7. Rest	8. Study	9. Study	10. Pre Test	11. Study	12. Study	13. Amy
14. Rest	15. Study	16. Exercise	17. Study	18. Study	19. FINAL	20. Rest
21.	22.	23.	24.	25.	26.	27.
28.	29.	30.	31.			

If you've been following all the strategies outlined in this book, then you've been studying all along. However, you do need to designate a certain amount of time prior to an exam to concentrate solely on studying for the exam using the strategies described in this chapter.

When planning your study schedule, you need to take into account the number of exams you are going to take, and the amount of time you have available before each one. If you are preparing for only one exam and you have plenty of time to study, you can be somewhat flexible in your schedule. However, if you are studying for several exams in a brief time period, you need to create a strict schedule for yourself and devote certain hours each day to the study of specific subjects.

In general, you should avoid studying too soon before the exam because you want the material you've prepared to remain fresh in your mind. At the same time, you need enough time to go over your notes, to prepare and work with the master lists, and to read additional sources and perhaps get help. To provide enough time to accomplish all this, you should begin studying about *five to seven days* before the examination.

You can divide your study preparation into several stages. The first stage, which you should do in one sitting, is to read through all your notes and create the master lists. Make certain you designate a large block of time (probably about four to six hours for each course) at the beginning of your study preparation period for this purpose.

The bulk of your study preparation should be devoted to working with the master lists, trying to memorize key terms and talking your way through possible essay questions. If you have the time, you can also read additional sources. Divide your day into blocks of time devoted to different tasks; you might, for example, spend the morning reading sources in the library, and the rest of the day working with the master lists.

If you are studying for more than one examination, make certain to study only one subject at a time, and give yourself a break of at least one hour before beginning to work on another; otherwise the material can easily become mixed together in your mind. Create a study schedule that divides your day into different study sessions with breaks in between. Each study session should be devoted to preparing for a single examination.

During the week prior to a major examination, it is extremely important that you get plenty of sleep and eat well. Your mind is doing some hard work, so let your body take a rest. You may feel you are getting a great deal accomplished by staying up late, but you are actually doing more harm than good. When you get over-tired, it becomes much more difficult to retrieve information from your long-term memory. If you arrive at an examination feeling exhausted, you won't be able to work through problems with a clear head.

The night before a major exam, you should give yourself a break and take it easy. However, that doesn't mean you should take the whole night off. Read over the master lists one final time to keep all of the information fresh in your mind, then watch TV or go to a movie. And make certain you get a good night's sleep.

IF YOU DO CRAM

The most effective way to study for an exam is to give yourself several days, ideally a week, in which to prepare. Of course, not everyone is able to do that all the time. If you do find yourself having to cram the day or night before a major test, do it wisely. The worst thing you can do is to pull an "all-nighter," drinking loads of caffeine to keep you awake. Even if you cover a great deal of material in those hours, you'll be so exhausted the next day you won't have the stamina to make it through the exam. You may know the material, but you won't have the energy to write a detailed essay, and your mind will be so foggy, you won't remember what you did study. You

Sample Study Schedule to Prepare for Major Exams: The Week Before Exams

	Mon.	Tues.	Wed.	Thurs.	Fri.	Sat.	Sun.
9-10:00		English Class	Gym/ Exercise	English Class	Gym/ Exercise	Work with History	Work with Psychology
10-11:00	Psych 101 Class	↓	Psych 101 Class	↓	Psych 101 Class	master lists	master lists
11-12:00	Meet with professors	Go to library to	Go to library to	Go to library to	Go to library to		
12-1:00	to ask about exams	read more on English	read more on History	read more on Biology	read more about Psych	↓	↓
1-2:00	L	U	N	C	H ———————————→		
2-3:00	Gym/ Exercise	Biology Class	Meet w/ study partners	Biology Class	Meet w/ study partners	Work with Biology	Meet with study
3-4:00	History Class	↓	History Class	↓	History Class	master lists	groups or go
4-5:00	Read over all	Read over all	Read over all	Read over all	Work with English	↓	to gym
5-6:00	English notes	History notes	Biology notes	Psychology notes	master lists		
6-7:00						Go to	Dinner
7-8:00	and create the three	and create	and create	and create	Make cue cards,	a movie and relax	Run through
8-9:00	master lists	master lists	master lists	master lists	quiz self, etc.		cue cards
9-10:00							
10-11:00	↓	↓	↓	↓	↓		
11-12:00	Relax, read, watch TV, go to bed by midnight						

Sample Study Schedule to Prepare for Major Exams: The Week of Exams

	Mon.	Tues.	Wed.	Thurs.	Fri.	Sat.	Sun.
9-10:00 10-11:00 11-12:00 12-1:00	Work with English and History master lists and cue cards; practice easy responses	Work again with Biology and Psychology lists and cards and notes	English Exam	Biology Exam			
1-2:00	**L**	**U**	**N**	**C**	**H**		
2-3:00 3-4:00 4-5:00 5-6:00	Work with Biology and Psychology master lists and cue cards; practice easy responses	Last run-through of English cards, lists, and notes	History Exam	Psych 101 Exam			
6-7:00	**D**	**I**	**N**	**N**	**E**	**R**	
7-8:00 8-9:00 9-10:00 10-11:00	Meet with study group or go to library for extra reading	Last run-through of History cards and notes	Last run-throughs of Biology and Psychology lists, cards, and notes				
11-12:00	Relax, watch TV, go to bed	Relax, watch TV, go to bed	Relax, watch TV, go to bed				

How to Skim a Text

In order to skim a text, read some or all of the following elements:

- Introductions and conclusions
- Summary paragraphs
- Chapter title and subtitles
- Any words or phrases that are bold, italicized, or underlined (If the terms are unfamiliar to you, read the entire sentence.)
- Captions for diagrams and photographs
- First and last lines of all paragraphs

NOTE: If a particular word, phrase, or line catches your attention and sounds significant, consider reading the entire paragraph.

can cram, but make certain you get at least four hours of sleep. The time spent resting will be more helpful to you than studying all night.

The smart way to cram is to read through all of your notes. But instead of making three master lists, make one on which you list only those terms, themes, or concepts that you don't

fully grasp. If you have the time, read through your notes twice; although you won't have the time to think through and memorize everything from the master lists, reading through your notes twice will at least expose you to the material. Another strategy is to take educated guesses and study only subjects that seem likely to turn up on an exam. Of course, this involves taking a gamble, but it might pay off.

If you haven't taken detailed notes from classroom lectures and reading assignments all semester, then you have more of a problem. It is extremely difficult at the last minute to catch up on all that material. If you've gotten yourself into this situation, then you should probably gamble and read only certain assignments carefully. If there's time, try to skim as many readings as possible (see the sidebar on this page on how to skim).

Remember, even if you are in this bad situation, you should still make certain you get some sleep. If you are well rested, you can at least call upon whatever background knowledge you have about the subject to help you in the exam.

ON EXAM DAY

The most crucial thing to remember on the day of the exam is to set your alarm and give yourself enough time to get yourself ready, especially if your exam is in the morning. More than one student has slept through a major exam, and it's hard to get sympathy from the professor when this happens. If your alarm is unreliable, or if you have the habit of turning it off in your sleep or hitting the snooze button, then set several alarms. You may even want to have a friend or relative give you a wake-up call.

When you take a shower that morning, try talking about some of the key terms or general themes you've prepared on the master list. This mental exercise serves to get your brain warmed up and focused on the subject matter. (Since you are in the shower, you won't feel awkward talking out loud.)

If your exam is in the afternoon or evening, you can read over your master lists in the morning. But don't overburden yourself. A final read-through should be all you need to put you in the right frame of mind for the exam. Don't spend this time trying to memorize or learn new material. After this read-through, do something to take your mind off the exam, such as taking a walk or watching TV.

On the day of the test, eat a high carbohydrate meal; carbohydrates, as many athletes know, give your body an energy boost. (A great meal to have before an exam is macaroni and cheese, because you get a mix of carbohydrates and protein.) Don't eat a large meal, though—that will make you sleepy.

Make certain you know exactly where the exam is being given and leave yourself enough time to get there. Try to get to an exam about fifteen minutes before it is scheduled to start; this will ensure you don't arrive late, flustered, and out of breath. You also want to have the benefit of the entire allotted time, from the first minute to the last.

Bring several pens of blue or black ink, or pencils and a sharpener if it is a standardized test, and a good watch. You might also want to bring some gum, candy, or a drink, if it is allowed. Make certain your watch is working or that there is a clock in the room: It is crucial to keep track of time during the exam.

When you get to the exam, choose your seat carefully. You might, for example, want to sit near a window so that you can look up every so often and take a break. You might want to sit where you can see the clock.

Before the exam begins, avoid talking about anything related to the test with other students, especially alarmists and panickers. You can sit at your desk and glance over your master lists or a last-minute cram sheet if you've made it. But don't get involved in a detailed question and answer session with other students;

it's really too late to learn any major point. Moreover, if you listen to someone else, you risk becoming confused about a point you were previously quite confident of. This will only serve to make you more anxious. Stay calm so you can take the exam with a clear head.

Study Schedule and Checklist

Before You Begin Studying (Before Classes End)

- Get information from the professor on exam content and format.
- Try to get sample tests.
- Find out date, time, and location of the exam.
- Consider joining a study group with other hardworking and intelligent students.

Five to Seven Days Prior to Exam

- Read through all notes from classroom lectures and reading assignments.
- Create the three master lists (key terms, general themes, and related concepts). Take four to six hours per subject to do this.

Two to Five Days Prior to Exam

- Work extensively and repeatedly with the master lists:
  - Quiz yourself on each master list for each subject every day.
  - Work with cue cards and use other memorization techniques to learn key terms.
  - Take notes on general themes and talk your way through possible essays.

Study Schedule and Checklist *(cont.)*

- See professor to ask last-minute questions if you have them.
- Meet with study group or partners, if you opt to do this.
- Read other sources, if time allows.
- Make certain you know where to go for the exam. Confirm the day, time, and location. If you are unfamiliar with the test site, go there before the test day so you can see exactly where it is and how much time it takes to get there.

The Night Before the Exam

- Give yourself one final read-through of the master lists.
- Talk your way through possible essays.
- Make a cram sheet of terms you still can't get down.
- Relax: See a movie or watch TV.
- Get together stuff to bring to the exam: pens (that work), watch (that works), candy, gum, a drink, your final cram sheet, and other materials you may need (such as a calculator, books, etc.).
- Get a good night's sleep.
- SET YOUR ALARM BEFORE GOING TO SLEEP!

The Day of the Exam

- Talk about some key terms and general themes in the shower for a mental warm-up.
- Eat a meal high in carbohydrates.
- If you have an afternoon or evening exam, use the morning for a final read-through of your master lists.
- Make certain you bring writing utensils and a watch to the exam.
- Get to exam early to choose a good seat.

FIGHTING THE ENEMY: WAYS TO COPE WITH PANIC

There's no question that preparing for and taking examinations is stressful. However, when stress becomes panic, it is a serious problem, one that plagues most students. Before an exam, panic can keep you from studying effectively; in the midst of an exam, it can mean the difference between success and failure.

Here are some strategies for fighting panic.

1. Have a Plan of Attack

One important antidote to panic is having a clear, well-thought-out plan of attack. Not having a plan is like going on a trip without a map—you worry about where you're going and, before you know it, you're lost. However, having a strategy to fall back on, you feel more in control of the situation and more confident of your abilities. You're probably thinking, "Great, where do I get a plan of attack?" You've got it already—the strategies you've been reading about in this chapter. So remind yourself that you have a plan of attack that will keep you on the path to exam success.

2. Remember the Big Picture

One major cause of panic is the tendency to blow the significance of exams completely out of proportion, to think of each exam as a matter of life or death. It's extremely important to put the experience into perspective by remembering the big picture. A single examination is only a small part of your overall educational experience and an even more minuscule part of your life. In future years, no one is ever going to ask how you did on a specific exam in school. You probably won't even remember the exam yourself. Moreover, doing poorly on an examination is not a reflection on you as a person. It's not even a reflection of intelligence. Some people are simply better at taking exams than others because they've developed successful test-taking skills—skills that you can learn also. Doing poorly on one exam does not mean you'll do poorly on others. But if you find you continue to do poorly, you can seek help. Most colleges, for example, offer special tutoring services. You can work regularly with a tutor and, most likely, improve your examination performance.

3. Avoid Alarmists

At all costs, stay away from the Alarmists. These are other students who, completely stressed out themselves, try to pass their panic on to you. What is truly alarming is how successful they can be at shaking your own confidence. Once they approach you and convey their own fears, you'll find you, too, are starting to get nervous. Panic is infectious; before you know it, you'll be freaking out right alongside them.

Be especially wary of rumors. Chances are what you hear about the level of difficulty of an upcoming examination or about specific questions are just rumors. If you let them sidetrack you from your own study preparations, you'll be wasting time.

Avoid Alarmists as much as possible, especially in the days before an exam. If an Alarmist corners you and asks how you feel about the exam, politely tell her you are studying as best you can and don't want to worry about what is on the exam until you get there.

You particularly want to avoid talking to Alarmists right before an examination begins. Many will get to the examination room early and ask fellow students to explain things they don't understand. There's really no point explaining various terms; this only gets everyone into a nervous frenzy just as the examination is being passed out. Don't talk about the test or the material with other people. The last thing you need to worry about before an exam begins is how much someone else understands. Stay calm and focus your thoughts on what you've already studied.

4. Take Breathers

Studying for, and taking examinations, is a physically and mentally exhausting procedure. It's crucial that you give yourself frequent breaks to help you relax. Don't study for more than two hours without taking a breather. Take a short walk, stretch your muscles. Even a ten- or fifteen-minute break can help you feel revived.

It's just as important that you take a breather while taking an examination. If you are not worried about the time, you can take a short break in the middle of the exam by asking to be excused to get a drink or go to the bathroom. If you don't want to leave the room, you can take a breather right at your seat. Put your pen down and give your hands a short rest. Take your eyes off the exam booklet and look out the window or around the room; just make certain you don't look anywhere near another person's paper, or you might be accused of cheating. Lift your arms in the air to stretch your back muscles and roll your head around to ease tension in your neck. Take several

really deep breaths. A breather like this only needs to take about thirty seconds, but it will help you remain calm and focused during the exam.

5. *Practice Relaxation Exercises*

There are many relaxation techniques that psychologists and therapists teach for coping with stress and panic. You can use these techniques while studying for exams and even while taking them. If you are particularly prone to stress, you may want to buy a book or tape that teaches relaxation exercises and practice them all semester.

Here is one basic technique that you can start doing right away. You should try to do this exercise a few times before an exam so that it will work more effectively during an actual test.

As you practice this exercise, you'll be able to experience that feeling of safety and happiness more and more quickly—in as little as thirty seconds—just by closing your eyes and breathing deeply. Even during an exam, you can take thirty seconds to close your eyes, breathe deeply, and relax.

Sit in a chair with a firm back and place your palms, face up, on the back of your knees. Close your eyes, and take deep breaths. Concentrate for a few moments only on your breathing, on the feeling of air going into and out of your lungs. Next, picture yourself someplace you've been where you felt safe and happy. See yourself there. Use all your senses. Remember the sights, smells, and sounds of being there. Think about this scene for several moments, continuing to breathe deeply. Enjoy the feeling of safety and serenity you know while you are there. At the same time, know that you can always return there, where you feel safe and happy, when you need to. Sit for as long as you like in this place. When you are ready to leave, count to ten, and then open your eyes.

TEST-TAKING STRATEGIES

BEFORE YOU BEGIN: LOOK AT THE BIG PICTURE

When you get the exam, don't just dive in and begin answering questions. Instead, take a moment to glance through the entire exam to see how it is structured and get a sense of the kinds of questions waiting for you. That way you can devise a plan of attack that ensures you use the time efficiently. Remember, having a plan of attack to fall back on minimizes the tendency to panic midway through the exam.

Look through the exam to see how many sections there are, the type of questions included, and the point values for each section. Then create a rough schedule for yourself allotting a certain amount of time for each section, depending on how many points it is worth and the level of difficulty.

Obviously, the more points a section is worth, the more time you should devote to it. For example, if an hour-long exam is divided into a short-answer section worth fifty points and an essay portion worth fifty points, then you should spend an equal amount of time for each section, thirty minutes. However, if the short-answer section is worth only thirty points, and the essay portion is worth seventy, then you should spend much more time on the essay section. You'd probably divide your time, with about forty minutes for the essay and twenty for the short-answer sections.

But you should also take into account the levels of difficulty of each section. For example, if you find short-answer questions much easier than essays, you can allot additional time to the essay portion of the exam.

The other advantage to looking at the entire exam beforehand is that you won't have any surprises waiting for you. It is extremely helpful, for example, to know if there is an essay section following the multiple choice questions. That way, while you are answering the multiple choice questions, you can also be thinking about how you will approach the essay. You might also come across short answer questions that include terms or give you ideas for things to include in the essay.

STRATEGIES FOR SHORT-ANSWER QUESTIONS

There are essentially three types of short-answer questions that are commonly asked on examinations: fill in the blank, true or false, and multiple choice questions. Although there are different strategies for each type of question, in general you can follow the same techniques.

1. Read the Directions

Students often make the mistake of diving right into the questions without reading the directions. The directions often include important information

you need to know *before* you start answering questions—that's why they're included on the examination in the first place. You may, for example, not be expected to answer all questions on the exam but have a choice. You won't know that, though, unless you read the instructions. It would really be unfortunate to take the time to answer all fifty questions, when the directions told you to choose only thirty. The directions might also indicate if you are penalized for incorrect answers. If you are penalized, then you won't want to guess as often. In general, get all the facts about the examination before jumping in.

2. Read Each Question Very Carefully and Watch for Trick Words

With all short-answer questions, it is extremely important that you read the question very carefully. Make certain you read the entire question and, if it is a multiple choice question, all the possible choices as well. Don't read the first few words or skim the question and think you know the answer. Sometimes the wording of a question (or the choices on a multiple choice question) will look familiar, and you'll therefore assume you know the answer; however, when you read the question carefully, you may find that even if an answer sounds right, it's still not.

When students get short-answer questions wrong, it's often the fault of "trick words" they've overlooked. These are crucial words tucked into the question that completely determine the correct answer but are easily overlooked.

For example, look at the following question:

Q. Which of the following is not by William Shakespeare?
   A. *Romeo and Juliet*
   B. *Troilus and Cressida*
   C. *Doctor Faustus*
   D. *Midsummer Night's Dream*
   E. *Love's Labours Lost*

If you read that question too quickly, you can easily skip over the word "not" and think it is asking you to identify a play that Shakespeare did write. And if you don't take the time to read all of the choices, you might first see Romeo and Juliet, know it is by Shakespeare, and assume that is the correct answer. However, if you read the question carefully, then you see the question is asking which play is *not* written by Shakespeare; that a small, three-letter word makes all the difference. And if you read all of the choices, you see there are three other plays in addition to *Romeo and Juliet*

that Shakespeare did write.

Here is a list of trick words frequently tucked into exam questions: *not, always, sometimes, never, all, some, none, except, more,* and *less.*

Always be on the lookout for these "trick words"; if you see one, underline it in the question so you can keep it in mind as you attempt to determine the answer. And never assume, just because a true or false statement, or a possible choice in a multiple choice question, looks familiar, that it is necessarily true or correct. There could be one word tucked in the sentence that invalidates the entire statement.

3. Watch the Time and Pace Yourself

Time is of the essence, especially on an exam. You don't have all day to mull over each question. You've therefore got to watch the clock and pace yourself to make certain you get to all the questions.

When you first get the exam, look at the total number of questions and how much time you have to answer them. You can then figure out approximately how much time you have to answer each one; of course, you may spend more time on the harder questions and less time on the easy ones, but it should average out. Check the time frequently. It's a good idea to get in the habit of checking your watch every time you turn the page of the exam. Monitor your progress and look at how many more questions you have to go. If you find you are going too slow, then try to pick up the pace.

Difficult questions will require more thought and therefore more time. When you get stuck on a particular question, you risk using up time that could be spent answering easier questions—the ones you immediately know the answers to, without a doubt. If you come across a very difficult question, skip it for the moment; that way you make certain you will get to all the questions you can answer easily and, therefore, get all those points. Put a circle around the difficult questions so you can find them when you go back. After completing all the questions you can answer without a problem, go back to the tricky questions and take the remaining time to work on them.

4. Intelligent Guessing

Chances are you are not going to know the answer to every single question on an examination; however, on a short-answer question, you can always take a guess. And if you guess intelligently, you have a decent shot at getting it right. Intelligent guessing means taking advantage of what you *do* know in order to try to figure out what you *don't*. It makes much more sense than random guessing.

GUESSING ON FILL-IN-THE-BLANK QUESTIONS

These are the most difficult to make guesses on because you need to furnish the answer; you aren't given a selection of choices as you are on a multiple choice question. You either know the answer or you don't. However, you can perhaps narrow down the possible answers by considering your master lists. Try to identify a general theme that the question reflects, and think about the key terms that relate to it. There's a strong

chance that one of those terms will be the correct answer. You can also look for, and underline, the key terms within the statement and think about the related concepts. Are the key terms in the statement part of a group of related concepts? What were the other key terms you listed in the same group? One of them is likely to be the right answer.

GUESSING ON TRUE OR FALSE QUESTIONS

It almost always pays to guess on these because you have a fifty-fifty chance of getting it right. If you are uncertain about the answer, test the statement by finding specific cases that support or counter it. For example, if the statement asserts that a particular phenomenon is always true, you only need to think of a single case when that statement is not true and the answer will be false. Similarly, if the word "never" or "sometimes" is included, you only need to think of a single case when the statement is true, and it will be false. When you come up with specific cases that support your guess, you can be confident your answer is correct.

GUESSING ON MULTIPLE CHOICE QUESTIONS

The key to guessing on these is to eliminate as many of the choices as you can. With each elimination, you raise the odds of picking a correct response. If you can narrow down to two choices, then you've got a fifty-fifty chance of getting it right—the same odds as on a true-or-false question.

There will usually be at least one choice you can eliminate right off the bat because it is obviously wrong. After that, examine each choice and see if there is anything incorrect within the answer itself. If the choice can't stand on its own as an accurate statement, then it is probably not a correct answer and you can eliminate it. For example, a possible choice might include a key term with the wrong definition. In that case, you know it won't be the right response. Finally, you can eliminate choices that don't reflect the same general theme as the question. A choice that relates to a completely different theme most likely will not be the correct answer.

Watch out for choices that, on their own, are correct and accurate statements; they aren't always the correct answer to the question. Just because a choice is itself an accurate statement doesn't mean it is correct in the context of the question.

Once you narrow down the responses to two options, don't spend too much time pondering and evaluating which one is the right choice. Just go with your gut instinct; these first impressions are usually right. And once you've put in your guess, don't go back and change it unless you later figure out the correct response with absolute certainty. Sometimes, for example, a later question will include information that sparks your memory or helps you figure out the answer to an earlier question. If that happens, go back and change the answer. Otherwise, forget about the question and forge ahead.

Many multiple choice questions include the options "all of the above" and "none of the above." When these statements are included, it becomes much easier to make a guess. Look at the other choices. If you identify one that you think is an accurate answer, you can confidently eliminate the "none of the above" option. By the same token, if you are only allowed to include one answer, and you find two choices that are accurate answers, the "all of the above" option must be the correct answer.

5. Visualizations

You might find, in the midst of an exam, that you've forgotten some piece of information you are certain you studied. This can be particularly frustrating because the answer is stuck somewhere in your long-term memory and you are having trouble accessing it. Close your eyes and try to picture the page from your notes or the master list on which the information is included. Try to "see" the page in your mind. Can you "read" the information on the page? Picture yourself studying those notes wherever you actually studied. Sometimes by seeing where you originally studied some piece of information, you can remember it. If none of that works, skip the question and move on to others. You may find that, as you answer other questions, you will remember the information you needed for an earlier one. Memory is a mysterious mechanism; sometimes it resists pressure until you are distracted.

6. A Word on Penalties

On some examinations, you are penalized more for putting in an incorrect answer than for leaving the question blank. On those tests, it won't pay to guess as often. However, if you can narrow down your choices to two or even three possibilities, it is usually to your advantage to guess, since the odds are in your favor. Additionally, if you get one "guess" right, you'll usually get enough points to outweigh several incorrect guesses.

7. If You Have Trouble Understanding the Question

Read over a difficult question a few times to see if you can at least get the gist of it. Don't worry about specific words you don't know. Focus, instead, on what the question is essentially asking. Does it want you to furnish a key term? Provide a definition of a term? Provide an example or illustration of some idea? Figure out the exception to some rule? If you can grasp the nature of the question, you may be able to narrow down the possible answers.

When you read over the question, underline any key terms. What general theme or topic is associated with those key terms? If you think more about that general theme, what related concepts or issues come to mind? Do any of these topics seem to tie into the question? If it is a multiple choice question, look at the various choices. Do you understand them? Do any of them contain key terms you are familiar with? Sometimes, even if you don't understand a specific question, you may be able to make a guess based on your overall knowledge of its general theme.

STRATEGIES FOR WRITING ESSAYS ON EXAMS

1. Read the Directions Very Carefully

Before you even begin to read the examination, make certain you read the general instructions. You need to find out, for example, how many essays you are supposed to write. Are you expected to answer all the questions, or do you have a choice? If there is a choice, how many essays do you need to answer? Are there any other requirements regarding specific things to include in your response? Requirements can seriously affect the way you approach essay questions, so it is essential you read them before you begin to write.

Sometimes, for example, teachers write lengthy essay questions that include more information than the actual question, such as quotations or anecdotes. Or there may be several questions related to a common topic, all of which you are expected to address in your response. There are also essay questions that are not even phrased as questions, but tell you to "discuss" or "address" some topic. Read carefully and try to identify exactly what you need to address in your essay. Underline any lines or phrases that specifically indicate points you are to consider.

2. Read the Questions Carefully

Don't begin writing until you have read the questions in their entirety and are certain you understand them. Essay questions will not always be written in a straightforward manner and you may have to think about what exactly is being asked of you.

3. If You Must Make a Choice

On many exams, rather than being given a single essay question, you will be given a choice of questions. Choose carefully, so you pick the question you can write the most impressive essay on. Don't just begin answering the first question. For each one, consider your knowledge of the topic and the specific points you would employ in an essay. You might even jot down a few notes next to each question, indicating your thoughts. Choose the question you have the most to say about, and feel most confident answering. Don't waste much time agonizing over the choices—time that could be spent actually writing. Look at the questions, think about each one, make your decision, and go with it.

Once you've made your decision, stick with it. Students sometimes lose their nerve halfway through their response and decide to try answering a different question. But by then they have little time left, making it difficult, if not impossible, to write an adequate response. You are generally better off sticking with your first choice and doing the best you can; even if you get stuck midway, you've probably written more than you could if you started on another. However, if you have a great deal of time left and find you truly cannot continue writing about a certain topic, then take the risk and switch questions.

4. Connect the Essay Question to a General Theme

When you consider how to respond to an essay question, first see if it connects with any of the general themes for the course; if it does, include the various points you studied in connection with each theme in the answer. If you are lucky, an essay question will mirror a theme you have studied almost exactly. However, it might not, and draw instead on several themes. If this is the case, you'll have to make some educated decisions about what to include and what to leave out.

The question might be phrased in such a manner that its relation to a general theme is not entirely apparent. In this case, look for any key terms in the question. Do they relate to a particular theme? If they do, the question probably relates somehow to that same theme.

5. If the Question Is Confusing or Difficult

It's always possible that you'll get a complex question that doesn't tie neatly into a particular theme. The professor may be trying to challenge you—to test your ability to grapple, on the spot, with a very difficult topic.

Examine the question and think carefully again about what is being asked. Remember, no matter how confusing the question looks, it must tie in somehow with the subject matter. Remind yourself that because you've spent a great deal of time immersed in this subject, you are equipped to discuss it. Look for any key terms or phrases you understand, and think about the general theme they relate to. You can sometimes discuss the general theme in a very broad sense and still get partial credit.

Whatever you do, make certain you always write *something*. If you panic and don't write anything, you are certain to fail; but if you write some kind of an answer, you can at least get partial credit. Everyone in the class is in the same boat, stuck with the same question and probably struggling with it as well. Try to write a confident, well-organized response based on course material, in which you address something that seems related to the question. You'll show the professor you learned something, and this should earn you some credit.

6. Jot Down a Few Notes

Once you've decided on an essay, jot down a few notes in the margin of the exam booklet on what you plan to address in your response. List the basic points, concepts, key terms, and examples you will raise; if you've identified a general theme that the question relates to, replicate the list of related topics you made at home. If this is not the case, brainstorm for a minute and write down your ideas.

Next, consider the order in which you will address them. An essay on an exam is no different from a term paper in that you should be strategic in your organization. Make certain to begin and finish with your most impressive points. But don't spend a great deal of time planning the essay; most of your time should be spent writing.

7. Neatness Counts—A Lot!

If your professor has to struggle to read your essay, he is not going to view it very positively, even if you've written a brilliant response. That's why, whether it's fair or not, neatness counts.

Use a black or blue ink pen, but not one that smudges easily. Only write on one side of a page in the exam booklet, since the ink can show through and make it difficult to read. Most importantly, write as neatly and legibly as possible. If your script is difficult to read, then write in print. It may take you a little longer to print, but your response will be neater and therefore worth the time it takes.

As you are writing, you may find you need to make changes—to cross out a line or a section, or add additional information to a previous paragraph. Make these changes clear. Cross out a section by drawing a line through the material; don't scribble over or blot out what you've written. To add a line or passage, write in the top margin of the page, circle the passage, and draw an arrow down to the spot where it should be inserted.

8. Communication Is the Key and You Are the Master

As you write, remind yourself you are writing for a specific audience with a specific purpose in mind—for your professor, to communicate how much you have learned about the subject. You want to make it crystal clear that you not only learned the material of the course, but have mastered it as well. That confident attitude should be reflected in the content and style of the essay.

You want to write, first of all, in as clear a manner as possible. If your ideas are confused, your wording will be confused also. Make certain you describe each point in detail. Anticipate any questions a reader might have, and answer them. Define any terms you use in explicit detail.

At the same time, adopt a tone that indicates your attitude toward the material. Use sophisticated vocabulary and terminology, but not in a forced or incorrect manner. Include as many relevant key terms as possible, along with explanations and definitions. You may even want to underline the key terms, so that they will stand out even if the professor skims the essay. Feel free to be a name-dropper and bring in other sources you may have read. Include as much relevant information as you can that will communicate the breadth of your knowledge and learning.

However, be careful. Don't, under any circumstances, include anything that is incorrect or that you don't fully understand. If you include any incorrect information, it will make a very poor impression and the professor may penalize you severely, even though other points are correct. You are better off leaving out a particular term or point altogether, if your use of it is incorrect. And while you want to convey the breadth of your knowledge, you don't want to pad the essay with irrelevant facts. You can include some that are related, but not central, to the essay, but don't throw in the kitchen sink. Don't bring up topics or terms that have nothing to do with the essay. If you do, the professor will think you don't really understand the question. Include only the points you know are relevant, and that will impress the professor.

9. Use a Three-Part Structure

Many students launch into an essay by writing whatever is on their minds, without any kind of structure or organization. This makes for a sloppy, unimpressive response that probably won't impress the professor. Even if a student raises intelligent points, they become lost if there isn't a solid structure to support them.

On an exam, however, you don't have much time to plan a detailed, complex structure. You can use the standard three-part structure—the same you would use for a term paper—that includes an introduction, body, and conclusion. This particularly lends itself to examination questions because it provides a set formula. You don't have to think about the organization; you merely plug the relevant information into those three parts.

THE INTRODUCTION

The introduction is particularly important on an examination because it provides your professor with the first sign of your knowledge of, and confidence in, the subject matter. If the introduction is clear and intelligent, the professor will gain a favorable impression that will remain with him as he reads on.

You don't, however, need to spend a great deal of time writing the introduction. It doesn't have to be especially innovative, creative, or lengthy—it only needs to be a single, short paragraph in which you establish the general topic of the essay. The simplest way to do this is to write a few sentences that essentially rephrase and expand on the question. You should also include a thesis statement that summarizes the central issue of the question (see pages 116–117 on Thesis Statements). Starting an essay this way not only provides you with material but, more importantly, it gets you writing.

The introduction can also be used strategically. Very often, there are several ways to interpret and approach a particular essay question. You can use the introduction to set the terms you plan to make your interpretation and approach with. If you make your intention clear from the beginning, your professor will tap into your thinking and see where you are going.

THE BODY

After the introduction, you should launch directly into the body of the essay. As with the essay as a whole, it is important the body be well organized and clearly structured. Make certain you divide the body into paragraphs, each centering on a specific point that supports the overall topic of the essay. If you've taken a few moments before the exam to jot down your ideas and plan the order in which you raise them, you should be able to write an organized body without too much trouble.

Whatever you do, don't turn in one long chunk of material that is difficult to read. Make certain the first line of each new paragraph is clearly indented. It's usually more effective in an exam to include many short

paragraphs rather than a few long ones, since it appears you are raising many different points. At the same time, make certain that each paragraph focuses on a very specific concept or example. If you include extraneous information, the essay appears unfocused and sloppy.

THE CONCLUSION

On an exam essay, the conclusion is as important as the introduction. Some professors only skim essays, especially if they have many to grade, but they usually read the introduction and the conclusion, so use these parts to your advantage. While the introduction provides the first impression, the conclusion is the final one your professor gets, and it comes right before he gives your essay a grade. You don't need to have an especially provocative or creative conclusion; you need only summarize the key points within the essay. This will show the professor that you successfully answered the question and know the subject matter. The conclusion doesn't have to be especially long, either—a few sentences will do. Make certain that you watch the time and leave yourself a few minutes to write it. If the exam ends when you are still working on the body, the essay is essentially unfinished and will appear tentative and unfocused. Adding a short conclusion demonstrates that you had a plan, and know where you were going.

10. Watch the Watch

Check the time frequently to be certain you have enough to get all the way through the essay. It's easy to get caught up in a single point, only to find time is running out and you have to rush through the rest of the response. Pace yourself and move quickly by giving yourself a certain amount of time to address each point and sticking to the schedule.

If you are running out of time, finish whatever point you are on and jump ahead to the conclusion. Make certain you include a conclusion, even if it is just a few sentences. In the conclusion, you might refer to some of the additional points you would have made if you had more time. This will at least let the professor know that you are aware of the information.

If you have so little time that you can't complete the essay or write a conclusion, make a brief outline listing the points you planned to address. The professor will see that you do know something about the subject and might give you partial credit. Include a brief note apologizing for not completing the essay because of lack of time. You might get some points for doing this— and every point counts.

Sample Essay Question and Response:

[Essay Question #1:] While many people consider the Middle Ages all to have been marked by the same general social character, there is a distinctive shift in the overall mood between the early and latter parts of the period. Write a well-developed essay in which you analyze the social and political changes in the latter half of the Middle Ages. In your answer, discuss how you would generally characterize the second half of the period.

In examining accounts of life in the Middle Ages, one detects a distinctive shift in tone between the earlier and latter halves of the period. While the earlier half is characterized by a tremendous optimism and hope in the future, the latter is marked by an increasing sense of gloom and despair. This shift in the general mood results in large part from the major social and political changes in the second half of the period.

Introduction:
— Restates the question in your own terms
— Makes clear your approach to the topic

The twelfth and thirteenth centuries, considered to be the early part of the Middle Ages, were marked by major political and economic developments that ushered in a time of relative stability. The ongoing struggles between the nobility and the throne were at last resolved during the reign of Henry II, who instituted major changes. Instituting a working bureaucracy, Henry successfully collected taxes and kept records of the incoming funds. The economy of the country was at last stabilized, and as trade increased with other countries, England grew richer. This ushered in a construction boom reflected in the rise in towns and cities, the building of the great cathedrals, and the formation of universities. This explosion of extraordinary achievements contributed to a general mood of hope and optimism in the future.

Body:
— Includes several major points supporting the topic

The latter half of the period, in the fourteenth and fifteenth centuries, however, was marked by a complete shift in mood. Instead of optimism and hope, it was a time of gloom and despair. There are several factors behind this shift. For one, the truce reached between the barons and the crown instituted by Henry II was once again threatened. Edward II and Richard II were comparatively weak kings, unsuccessful at standing up to the nobles. During their reigns, the country was constantly beset by civil war. Both kings were eventually deposed by nobles.

In addition to civil wars, the One Hundred Years' War (1337-1433) was a long, debilitating war. The war began when Edward III claimed he had a right to the French throne through his mother. Although the war was fought entirely on French soil, the English economy was seriously depleted. While people back home were going hungry, bands of English soldiers were ravaging and pillaging the French villages and cities. The war was therefore controversial and very unpopular among many people who saw it as unnecessary. After a series of disastrous battles, the English withdrew and gave up all their claims in France.

—Each paragraph centers on a single point

— Mentions many key terms, which are defined and explained

Another major event that changed the mood was the Black Plague in 1348. The plague spread with astonishing speed and killed off about one third of the general population—a staggering amount. This was responsible in part for creating economic problems. Most of those killed by the plague were poor people; the nobles largely escaped it. There was therefore a major shortage of labor. All building had to stop and farming seriously declined, creating food shortages. In addition to economic problems, the plague generally fostered a sense of despair. People saw death everywhere around them, and became obsessed with it. This is evident in the art and literature of the period, which features the figure of Death in various forms. The *Danse Macabre*, for example, features death striking down various members of society, regardless of age or class.

     Finally, the church instigated a new policy that brought about a major change in people's attitudes toward it. In the fourteenth century, the papacy condoned the sale of pardons and indulgences. The sale was a way you could essentially buy penance for sins you had committed. This meant, in part, that those with money could buy their way into heaven easily, while the poor could not. It also led to a great deal of church corruption, since those selling pardons could blackmail innocent people into buying their wares. In Chaucer's *Canterbury Tales*, the Pardoner is a typical example of a corrupt church official, reflecting the general view among the public of the church in the period. Additionally, many church offices began to be auctioned off to the highest bidder, or went to family members of existing officers. As a result, the general populace began to feel more and more skeptical of the church as a moral institution.

— Written in a confident, knowledgeable tone

The fourteenth and fifteenth centuries thus saw several major negative social and political developments, including the threat to the throne under weak kings, the Hundred Years' War, the Black Plague, and increased church corruption. There were other developments as well, including a series of popular rebellions waged by the exploited lower classes that were often put down in violent fashion by the throne. The combination of economic turmoil and the harsh reminders of sudden death all around them quite naturally led people to feel despair and gloom. This marks a sudden shift from the general optimism of the earlier half of the Middle Ages, when political and economic stability and prosperity had led to great changes.

Conclusion:
— Restates the main points addressed in the essay clearly and concisely
— Mentions additional, related topic not addressed (due to lack of time)
— Clearly indicates the essay is completed

After the Exam

Exams can give you valuable insights into your strengths and weaknesses as a test-taker. Whenever possible, examine your tests after they've been graded. If the exam was given during the school semester, your professor will probably give it back to you. If the exam was a final, you may need to make an appointment with the professor and ask to see it. Your finals are especially important in preparing your strategy for next semester.

When you get the exam, look through it and study any errors you've made. First, make certain you understand why you got points off. It's particularly important that you do this if later examinations in the semester will cover the same material. If you don't get these points right the first time, you're not going to get them right on the final.

At the same time, try to identify patterns to your errors. Is there a particular type of mistake you made? Did you tend to make factual errors, failing to identify and define key terms correctly? Or were your errors more conceptual, involving the way you approached problems and questions? Did you misread or misunderstand the questions? If you can pick out a pattern, you can focus on that particular problem and work to make changes.

You can also try to talk to your professor about the exam. Ask for advice about what you might do in the future to raise your grade. You should talk to the professor particularly if you have failed the exam. By doing this, you demonstrate that you are not a lazy or uncaring student and that you take the grade seriously. With luck, the professor might offer valuable advice on how to study that will help you on future tests.

Sometimes teachers do make mistakes when they grade exams. If you catch an error, think first about whether it's worth pointing out to the professor. Because you create an unfavorable impression, it's generally not worth quibbling over a few points—even if you get them, the professor may be less inclined to give you a high grade for the course. If there was a serious error made in grading your exam, by all means point it out. However, you should only do this if you are absolutely certain the professor made a mistake. If you challenge a grade and you are not correct, the professor will not take kindly to it.

If you did poorly or failed, don't get too down about it. Remember this one exam is a small part of a much bigger picture. Later in your life, no one will know what grade you got on a specific test back in school; you probably won't remember it yourself. Try, as much as you can, to turn it into a learning experience; even if you fail a test, you gain some knowledge that can help you in the future.

Important Points to Remember

1. Studying means thinking and working, not passively reading.

2. Know what you're in for; get as much information about an upcoming exam as possible.

3. Get help if you need it.

4. Stay healthy; maintaining a sound mind and body helps improve performance on examinations.

5. Use whatever strategies you need to in order to fight panic.

6. Guess intelligently; use what you do know to figure out what you don't.

7. Take examinations strategically; keep a clear head, watch the time, and pace yourself.

8. Read all questions carefully; make certain you understand them. Try to translate difficult questions into everyday, conversational speech.

9. Learn something from each test you take that can help you on future exams.

CHAPTER 6

Secrets of Study Success

SUCCESSFUL STUDYING: MAKING IT A HABIT

In previous chapters, we've examined strategic approaches to specific study tasks. But there's more to being a student than these individual duties. In addition to the way you approach these study tasks, you've got to adopt an effective study routine for everything you do. In this chapter, you'll read about the various habits you should make part of your study routine.

As a student, you are faced with so many tasks and responsibilities, it can seem overwhelming. The key to making it all manageable is making it all a matter of habit. The more routine something is, the less effort it requires. Think about your morning routine. You probably go through the same ritual every day—showering, brushing your teeth, taking vitamins—without thinking about it. If you also make study tasks a habit, they'll come as easily as brushing your teeth.

However, you must adopt the right habits. After all, not all habits are necessarily good. At the beginning of each previous chapter, you saw examples of the wrong ways to approach various study tasks that can easily become habits. Once a habit is set, it becomes hard to break. By making the strategies and approaches outlined in this book a part of your general study routine, you guarantee you will adopt the right habits.

GETTING ORGANIZED

When you're a student, studying becomes your job. But being a student is tougher than most nine-to-five office jobs because your responsibilities and duties are constantly changing. Every day, every week, every month, and every semester present new assignments and tasks, and if you don't keep track of them, you'll find that your work—and your life— become a complete mess.

That's why it's essential that you organize yourself right from the start. Before you begin classes, buy a pocket date book or calendar for keeping a record of all your responsibilities. Note the deadlines for assignments, exam dates, appointments with professors or study partners, and extracurricular activity meetings, as well as any other obligations. Get in the habit of carrying your date book around with you so you can make additions or changes at any time. For example, you might arrive at class one day and find out that the professor has decided to change the date of the midterm exam. You can put the new date right in your calendar. That way you're certain not to forget it.

In addition to keeping careful records of your responsibilities in your date book, you should also make an effort to keep all your notes and study materials neatly organized. There's not much point in taking notes if they wind up in a crumpled pile of paper at the back of your desk. Keep your notes clearly labeled and organized. Find a space you can designate as your study area, where you keep all the study materials—notes, textbooks, articles—that you need for the semester. That way you'll be able to quickly find anything you need.

On the Shelf: Reference Books You Should Own

There are certain reference guides that every student should own, and they are well worth the investment. These books prove themselves indispensable at various times, from helping you to write essays and papers to enabling you to look up additional information as you read required texts and your classroom notes.

- **A Collegiate Dictionary**—This is the most important reference book for a student to own. As you go about your required reading for courses, you'll encounter many new vocabulary words you'll need to know in order to follow what you read. Additionally, as you write essays, you should double-check the spelling and meaning of any words for which you are not 100 percent certain of the correct usage.

- **A Thesaurus** (preferably in dictionary format)—This is a resource for improving your writing. By looking up synonyms for frequently used words, you can alter your usage with synonyms and antonyms and make your writing much more interesting.

- **A Specialized Dictionary**—There are many of these dictionaries on the market that list words, names, and terms within specific fields, such as literature, science, philosophy, and mythology. Depending on what areas you study, you may wish to purchase one or several of these guides.

- **A World Atlas**—You'd be surprised how much information you can get from a good atlas. As you read or write, you can dip into it for various facts, from identifying capitals to basic information about countries. As you come across a place name in your reading, you can enhance your sense of it and of its place in the world by opening your atlas.

On the Shelf: Reference Books You Should Own *(cont.)*

- **A Grammar Handbook**—Turning in essays that are grammatically correct is extremely important; using proper grammar tells your teacher that you are a serious student who takes pride in your work. There are, of course, so many different rules and exceptions to the rules that it is difficult to know them all by heart. If you own a good grammar handbook, you can dip into it and double-check any rules that give you trouble.

- **A Style and/or Essay Format Manual**—In addition to writing with proper grammar, it is also important that you are consistent in your style and format. Be consistent first and foremost with how you cite outside sources and list them in your bibliography. Depending on which format your teacher instructs you to follow, make certain you purchase a format guide, such as the MLA or APA handbooks. Also, be consistent throughout your writing with punctuation and language usage. A style book such as *The New York Times Manual of Style and Usage* will provide assistance in these matters.

- **An Almanac**—Owning an almanac may seem silly, but you'll be surprised how much useful information it contains. You never know when you'll need some tidbit for a paper you're writing. Dip into the almanac for looking up miscellaneous facts and figures, from past Academy Award winners to a list of the U.S. presidents and their birthplaces.

TIME MANAGEMENT: MAKING A STUDY SCHEDULE

Many study guides instruct you to set a rigid schedule for yourself in which each minute of each day is devoted to fulfilling a certain task. These schedules block off time for everything from study sessions to mealtimes to hours when you can sleep. But schedules like these are virtually impossible to stick to. What if, for example, you don't feel like eating dinner at exactly 6:30 on a particular night? What if you are supposed to study from 8:00 to 11:00 on Tuesdays, but one week your professor wants you to attend a guest lecture at the same time? What if there is a really good party on a Wednesday night you want to go to, but you don't have time scheduled for it? What do you do?

Student life is far too chaotic to be squeezed into a neat, orderly schedule. Your schedule will change frequently: One week you may have a major exam or a paper due, which will require more work, while another week, you may have to devote substantial time to an extracurricular activity. Even weekly study tasks, such as reading lecture notes or assigned texts, will take different amounts of time. One week the assigned readings may be very difficult and take twelve hours to complete, while another they'll be substantially easier and only take four hours. But if you are stuck in a rigid schedule, you won't be able to make the necessary adjustments to provide the time you need.

However, you do need to have some kind of schedule so that you can keep track of what needs to be done and leave yourself enough time to do it. Instead of making a rigid schedule, you can plan a more general one that will allow you to make changes on a week-to-week and day-to-day basis.

This general schedule only shows those activities you do every week of the semester at the exact same times. You should make it up at the beginning of the semester, before classes have actually started. Make a chart listing days of the week at the top, and the hours of the day in a column on the left side. First, find out the meeting times of all your classes, and block off those times on the schedule. Then mark off any times you will be consistently unavailable to study; for example, those times when you are part of a club or a team will definitely be busy.

After you've blocked off those hours, you'll be able to see the times each day that are "free." Those "free" times can be spent any number of ways—studying, doing work, socializing with friends, etc. You can decide each week exactly how you can best utilize those "free" times.

Sample General Schedule

	Mon.	Tues.	Wed.	Thurs.	Fri.	Sat.	Sun.
9-10:00		English		English			
10-11:00	Psych 101		Psych 101		Psych 101		
11-12:00							
12-1:00							
1-2:00	Sociology		Sociology		Sociology		
2-3:00		Biology		Biology			
3-4:00	History		History		History		
4-5:00							
5-6:00	Gym		Gym		Gym		Gym
6-7:00							
7-8:00	Literary Magazine		Literary Magazine				
8-9:00							
9-10:00							
10-11:00							

Sample General Schedule with "Free" Times Marked Off

	Mon.	Tues.	Wed.	Thurs.	Fri.	Sat.	Sun.
9-10:00		English		English			
10-11:00	Psych 101		Psych 101		Psych 101		
11-12:00							
12-1:00							
1-2:00	Sociology		Sociology		Sociology		
2-3:00		Biology		Biology			
3-4:00	History		History		History		
4-5:00							
5-6:00	Gym		Gym		Gym		Gym
6-7:00							
7-8:00	Literary Magazine		Literary Magazine				
8-9:00							
9-10:00							
10-11:00							

= "Free" time

Note: "Free" times can be used to study, read required texts, do homework, eat, relax, and socialize.

This is your general schedule that indicates the times you have commitments and the times you are "free" in a given week. But each week presents its own specific tasks and requirements that you should plan for. At the start of each week, sit down and make a list of all the tasks that must be completed; this includes reading assignments, going over lecture notes, researching and writing essays, preparing for major exams, and working on school projects. If you have other things to do that week, include those on your list as well. For example, you may have to attend a special event or an extracurricular meeting.

After you've made up your list of specific tasks for the week, go down the list and designate days and times to work on each task, making certain they are within the "free" blocks on the general schedule. You don't need to set exact times for each task; you can simply write down the day and general time you plan to spend doing it. You may, though, want to estimate how long each task will take to complete so that you block out an appropriate amount of time.

✔ Read Articles for Psych	Sun., Tues. Evenings (2 hrs.)
✔ Read Chapters 1-5 of Huck Finn	Mon. Evening (1–2 hrs.)
✔ Read Chapters 5-10 of Huck Finn	Wed. Evening (1–2 hrs.)
✔ Study for Bio Quiz on Thursday	Tues., Wed. Night
✔ Meet with Group to work on project for Soc.	Sun. Afternoon (4 hrs.)
✔ Read Chapter 14 for Sociology	Tues. Evening (1 hr.)
✔ Finish Poem for Lit. Magazine	Mon.–Wed. Night (after 11 P.M.)
✔ Go over Notes from Lectures, Readings	Sat. (4 hrs.)
✔ Library Research for Soc. project	Mon.–Thurs. Midday (between classes)

During the week, work on each specific task during the time you've designated. However, don't force yourself to spend an exact amount of time on each one. Take each task as it comes; some will take longer than you anticipate, some will take less. Just make certain that by the end of the week you've fulfilled all the tasks you set for yourself.

You will have to read assigned texts and go over lecture notes every week, and you will probably want to work on those tasks during the same general times each week. For example, you may want to read assignments for a certain class on the same night each week so that it is completed before class the next day. Don't block off specific times to the minute, however, because the reading will take varying amounts of time.

In addition to making a weekly list of specific tasks, it's a good idea to make one for each day. Before you go to sleep each night, you can quickly make a list of the things you need to do the following day. You can include, in addition to study tasks, any specific errands you need to run, from doing laundry to returning books to the library. That way, you've got all your tasks in one place and you won't forget to do something. As you do each one, cross it off the list so you can see yourself making progress and feel you are accomplishing something.

Of course, everyone needs time away from work; but you shouldn't "schedule" in these times. As a student, your priority is fulfilling your study requirements, as well as commitments to extracurricular activities. These will take up a certain portion of time each week. When they are completed, any time that remains is yours to do with as you please.

For example, if you've designated Tuesday evening as the time to read for your Psychology class, you may find that you've finished the reading by 9 P.M. If you have no other tasks designated for that day, then you can do whatever you want with the remaining time. Expect to have less personal free time during weeks when you have exams or major papers and projects due. But always factor in plenty of time for sleep!

There will be some weeks when you have an especially heavy work-load and face a severe crunch for time.

To prioritize your tasks, look at your list for the week and try to put them in order of importance. For example, completing an assignment that must be handed in or studying for a major exam are going to take priority over most other activities.

After identifying what is most important for that week, make certain you devote most of your time to fulfilling those tasks. If you finish them, spend the remaining time on the less important ones. If you don't get to the less important tasks, you can make up for it in later weeks when the workload is less heavy. Just be certain you catch up at some point so you don't have a heavy workload right before exams.

REWARDS AS MOTIVATION

You're not going to want to study every time you are supposed to. Nevertheless, you're going to have to motivate yourself somehow to do work even if you don't feel like it. One way to do this is to reward yourself when you accomplish specific study tasks.

Any time left after you've completed your study tasks for a particular day is your personal free time. This in itself serves as a reward to get you motivated to work. For example, if you know you want to watch television at night, you can force yourself to work efficiently during the day. Similarly, if you want to go to a party on the weekend, you'll try your hardest to get all your work done during the week. You just need to remind yourself of the fun activities waiting for you when you are finished working.

However, even with the promise of free time as a reward, you may still find it difficult to get motivated and begin working. You can provide yourself with additional rewards as you study. Set small goals, and reward yourself each time you fulfill them. For example, if you have several hours blocked off on Tuesday night for reading forty pages, promise yourself a snack after you've gotten halfway through the assignment. This will at least get you started.

These rewards don't need to be extravagant. A reward can simply be a short break to do something you like—getting ice cream, talking on the phone, going for a walk, listening to music, whatever. Just make certain the "reward" time is a short break lasting no more than twenty to thirty minutes.

This rewards system is particularly helpful if you have to spend long hours at work, such as studying for an exam or writing a paper. If you think of yourself as slaving away for many long hours, it will be extremely difficult to motivate yourself to begin work. However, if you divide the task into several smaller ones and promise yourself a small reward at the completion of each one, it will be much easier to get started. You know then that when you sit down to work, a reward of some kind is not all that far away.

When you finish a major task, such as completing an essay or taking a final exam, it's nice to give yourself a bigger reward—a new CD or a fun evening out. These rewards will help you get through the especially difficult work periods during the school year.

Your Teacher Is Smarter Than You Think

Some students think they can easily outsmart the teacher. Keep in mind, though, that your teacher was once a student, too. Any tricks you think of, your teacher has probably thought of, too.

There is a popular story passed on from one student to another about an incident that supposedly took place at an American college. As the story goes, four college buddies decided to take a weekend ski trip, even though they had a major exam coming up that Monday afternoon.

They had a great weekend partying but, on their way home Monday morning, they realized none of them had studied. They decided to skip the exam and make up an excuse.

When they went to class the following Wednesday, they told the professor they had been driving to class Monday morning from their off-campus apartment, when they'd gotten a flat tire several miles away from school. They tried to fix it as fast as they could, they said, but the flat detained them for several hours and forced them to miss the exam. The professor expressed sympathy for their plight and told them they could make up the exam that Friday. The four friends were thrilled that they got all this extra time to study.

They showed up at the classroom Friday completely prepared for the exam. The professor passed out the test and when the four friends turned over the exam, they were horrified to find this one question: Which tire on your car had the flat?

FINDING A COMFORTABLE STUDY SPACE

Many people seem to think that the only way to study is at a bare desk, with a hard-backed chair, in some minuscule study cubicle in the library. While this setting does wipe out any outside distraction, it's such a gloomy, sterile atmosphere that it turns studying into a form of medieval torture. Studying just doesn't have to be that depressing.

Since you will spend long hours at the books, reading over your notes and assigned texts, you may as well make yourself comfortable. If you work in a space where you are relaxed and feel at home, you will study more often and more effectively. Study anywhere you feel comfortable—in your room, in bed, at the library, in an empty classroom, at a café,

outside, in the park—provided that you do two things: (1) Minimize outside distractions; and (2) promise yourself to make a change if you don't get the work done.

In choosing a place, consider the amount of outside distraction—such as friends stopping by, the phone ringing, loud music—and do what you can to minimize it. Even the library may not be distraction-free; if everyone you know goes there to study, you may spend more time chatting with friends than studying. You can, though, minimize the distraction by avoiding the main study lounge and finding a quieter section of the library, where you won't run into many people you know.

There's nothing wrong with studying in your room so long as you get work done.

Your room is, after all, the space where you are most at home. However, you will need to minimize distractions. If you are frequently interrupted by the phone, turn the ringer off; if friends frequently disturb you, keep the door closed.

If you decide to study in your room, it's a good idea to designate a spot as your main work space. Your desk is probably the best place. However, your room need not have a sterile, austere atmosphere. Since it's your room, you can personalize it by hanging up posters or photographs.

You can even listen to music while you study, just as long as it doesn't distract you. Listening to something old that you are very familiar with will distract you less than something brand new. If you study outside your room, you can try bringing a walkabout tape or CD player along and listening to relaxing music. That's one way to make wherever you study feel a little more like home.

Whatever study space you choose, try to do most of your work there. This will help make studying more of a habit. Arriving at that space—whether it's your desk in your room or your favorite spot in the library—alerts you to the fact that it is time to work. You can begin work more easily in a familiar setting than you can in a strange environment.

You can also designate different places for different study tasks. For example, you might decide to read assignments for class at home, but go over lecture notes in the library. Studying in a variety of locations does make the process less tedious. However, you should make it a habit to do the same study tasks in the same place so they will seem more routine.

Sometimes, for whatever reason, you'll find it difficult to pay attention. When this happens, a simple change of scene may be all you need to refocus on your work. If you've been studying at your desk, go out somewhere, to a coffee shop or the library, and see if you get more done. However, if you find you consistently don't get a great deal of work done, make a more permanent change. If, for example, you are so relaxed studying in your room that you always fall asleep, then that's probably not the best place for you to work.

Remember, pick a work space where you feel relaxed and comfortable, but one where you also get work done. This means being honest with yourself. Only you know whether you are studying effectively; if you aren't, then you need to initiate changes.

No Time to Nap: Staying Awake While You Study

It might sound like a joke, but falling asleep while reading or studying is a problem that plagues many students. The need to sleep is powerful—and to fight it, you need to take equally strong measures. Here are a few important suggestions.

- **Get Enough Sleep at Night.** There's a simple reason why so many students fall asleep while studying, and it's not necessarily boredom. They're just tired. Of course, it's difficult when you are a student to get a good night's sleep all the time, and you shouldn't expect to. However, don't make a habit of staying up late all the time. Try as often as possible to get six to eight hours of sleep a night.

- **Don't Get Too Much Sleep.** You might not realize it, but there is such a thing as *too much sleep*. For most people, six to eight hours of sleep a night is sufficient. If you get more sleep than your body needs, you can feel sleepy all day long.

- **Exercise Regularly.** If you exercise regularly, you'll sleep better at night and be more energized during the day. That means you'll be more focused on your classes and your studies.

- **Become Alarmed.** If you tend to fall asleep while studying, set an alarm. You can purchase an inexpensive travel clock or wristwatch equipped with an alarm and have it nearby while you study. The alarm should be loud enough to wake you up but quiet enough not to disturb those around you. If possible, set the alarm to go off every fifteen minutes. If you can't set it to go off regularly, set it for a specific time (such as a half hour after you've begun studying) and continue to reset it each time it goes off.

No Time to Nap: Staying Awake While You Study *(cont.)*

- **Wake-Up Calls/Visits.** If you don't trust an alarm, have a friend check on you every so often. The easiest method is to arrange to study together; that way you can both keep an eye on the other and keep each other awake. Of course, you have to be careful that you both don't fall asleep at the same time, and also that you don't spend too much time chatting. If you are studying in your room, you can have a friend or relative give you a phone call every hour or so to check up on you.

- **Take Breathers.** If you become too comfortable while studying, it's easy to fall asleep. You should plan to get up and walk around at regular intervals—preferably outside. While fresh air can do wonders for waking you up, limit your walks to just five minutes. When you return to studying, you'll feel revived and better able to focus.

- **Stay Actively Involved.** The more engaged in the material you are, the less likely you'll succumb to sleep. Rather than just reading the words on the page, have a conversation with yourself in your mind about what you read; read a few lines and then comment on them.

- **Don't Get Too Comfortable.** It's important to be comfortable while you study because the more relaxed you are, the more open your mind will be. Additionally, being comfortable makes studying less tedious. However, there is such a thing as being too comfortable. If you find yourself constantly falling asleep, you should change your study habits. For example, if you study on a couch or bed, you might need to sit at a desk, where it is more difficult to fall asleep. If you listen to music, you might need to change your selection to something that will keep you up rather than lull you to sleep. Remember, study in an atmosphere you feel relaxed in, but not so much that you cannot stay awake.

Go with the Tide, Not Against It

Some guidebooks claim there are optimum times and places for studying, and that all students should follow the same schedule. But not all students are alike. One might be a morning person who works most efficiently in the early hours, while another is a night owl, whose best work is produced after midnight. One might study efficiently in the library, while another works best lying on the couch in the dorm lounge. It's therefore foolish to think all students should study in exactly the same way according to the same schedule. In fact, forcing yourself to follow a schedule that doesn't suit your personality makes the process less effective and much more tedious than it needs to be.

General approaches to studying need to be tailored to suit your individual personality. Don't go against this tide. Determine what kind of student you are and in which conditions you work best, and use that information to determine your study routine. Learning what kind of student you are takes time, as well as some trial and error. Make it a habit to question the effectiveness of your study habits. Are you working as efficiently as possible? Are you accomplishing the tasks you set for yourself each week? If you are having trouble, it could be time to make a change.

Eventually, you should find yourself falling into a comfortable routine that helps you accomplish all the goals you set for yourself.

BY THE BOOK

No matter what course you take or what you major in, a majority of a student's duties center on reading and writing. These skills play a vital part in completing assignments for classes and taking examinations. Fortunately, you improve these skills as you do them more frequently—even outside of class to improve even further.

Try making it a habit to read more frequently during your free time. Read newspapers, magazines, fiction, or non-fiction. Just by reading frequently, you become more accomplished at it. You will also learn all kinds of miscellaneous facts that you might be able to use in your studies at some point. Even a trashy novel might have something to teach you: A courtroom thriller could teach you something about the law; a romance novel, set in a country you've never visited, may teach you about foreign customs. Of course, you may not learn anything monumental; but even small things can be useful or simply interesting.

You can also work on improving your vocabulary. Almost any time you sit down to read, you'll probably encounter some new word (even in trashy bestsellers). Try to look up one new word that you've never heard before each time, and you'll steadily build your vocabulary. You can use these new words in essays. Moreover, you'll find that as your ability to read and interpret texts improves, so will your ability to read and interpret test questions.

Studies have shown that reading frequently also improves one's writing abilities. The more you read, the more comfortable you feel with language. As a result, you gain more of an instinct for what is written correctly; as you write, something will simply "sound right" or "sound wrong."

In addition to reading, you might also consider keeping a journal. You can write down anything you wish in a journal—poetry, your thoughts and feelings, accounts of things you've done or accomplished, descriptions of things you've seen or overheard. You don't ever have to show the journal to anyone, so you don't have to worry about grammar or spelling. Just write whatever or however you like. If you write in a journal frequently, you'll become more comfortable writing in general, more accustomed to setting your thoughts down on paper.

Word Power

Here's a list of words you can use in your writing and conversation that are guaranteed to make you sound smarter. For each word, you'll find a concise definition and an example of the word used in a sentence. After you've mastered these words, be on the lookout in your reading for additional vocabulary you can learn and put into use. Remember that the key to learning new words is using them frequently.

evince. To display clearly, show, or reveal.
> *A detailed study of these two plays will* evince *many similarities between them.*

formulate. To put into a set statement or expression, to devise (as in a policy or plan).
> *The novel's theme is* formulated *in the final chapter.*

fortuitous. Lucky, happening by chance, accidental.
> *It was certainly* fortuitous *that they ran into each other in London.*

germane. Relevant, appropriate to, fitting.
> *A discussion of bone structure is certainly* germane *to our study of anatomy.*

hegemony. Those persons or institutions in power over others.
> *The church was a* hegemonic *institution in the Middle Ages.*

heinous. Shockingly evil and hateful.
> *Richard III is the most* heinous *of Shakespeare's villains.*

illuminate. To make clear, shed light on.
> *This paper will* illuminate *the specific connections between the author's life and work.*

ingenuous. Showing innocent and childlike simplicity and candor; noble and honest, trusting.
> *She is so* ingenuous, *she will trust just about anyone.*

Word Power *(cont.)*

juxtapose. To place side by side for the sake of comparison.
If we juxtapose a painting by Van Gogh with one by Matisse, their similar use of color becomes clear.

manifest. To make evident or certain by showing or displaying.
His concern for the underprivileged has been made manifest many times by his extensive volunteer work.

ontological. Relating to the nature of existence and our knowledge of it.

Her writings have taken an ontological twist now that she has begun to discuss more personal issues.

perspicacity. Acute mental power; shrewdness.
Your adept performance in that oral examination demonstrated your perspicacity.

plethora. An abundance or excess.
To prove my point, I will raise a plethora of sources and pieces of evidence.

praxis. Customary action or practice.
It is usually easier to understand something in praxis rather than theory.

preponderance. A majority; a superiority in power, importance, number, or strength.
In the election, she had a preponderance of devoted followers.

prevalent. Widespread, generally accepted, seen, or favored.
Signs that the economy is not doing well are certainly prevalent.

There's no way around the fact that grades are a central part of most schools. A large portion of a grade is based on objective information, such as the number of short-answer questions you got right or wrong or the number of days you attended class. However, grading is also subjective: It is based in large part on the teacher's impression of you. While this impression can't change the number of exam responses you got right or wrong, it can influence other aspects of your final grade. For example, a final grade will often reflect a grade for class participation, which is much more difficult to measure than the number of right or wrong responses.

It is extremely important that you try to make a good impression. However, you also need to be careful how you do it. If you overdo your effort, it can seem insincere and backfire. For example, if you interrupt the lecture or class discussion simply to make some comment that demonstrates how smart you are, you will not impress the teacher. Moreover, the teacher might resent that you've interrupted class for a non-related point in an obvious attempt to gain Brownie points.

The impression you want to convey is not necessarily how smart you are, but that you are a conscientious student who is willing to work hard to learn. There are several specific things you can do to make this impression.

PERFECT ATTENDANCE

Nothing is more off-putting to a teacher than a student who consistently comes late to class, or doesn't come at all. Coming late disrupts the entire class and, more severely, indicates to the teacher that you don't care about the class. Even in a large lecture course, where you think you might slip in unnoticed, a teacher can notice a student who arrives late. You should therefore make it a habit to get to class on time. If you have a special reason for being late, make certain you see the professor during office hours to explain the situation and apologize.

Coming late to class is a disruption; not coming at all is a major problem that can seriously affect your grade. In some smaller classes, a teacher will take attendance. If this is the case, you should obviously make certain you go as often as possible. Having perfect attendance will probably impress the teacher when it comes time to make your class participation grade.

Even if a teacher does not take attendance, it is still worth going to class as often as you can. For one thing, being there on a regular basis ensures that you are exposed to all the course material, which in itself will probably improve your grades. Moreover, if you attend class regularly, the teacher will consider you a familiar face.

OFFICE VISITS

If a teacher doesn't know you by name, however, it won't matter what image she has of you when she gives you a grade. While a teacher will usually know you by name in a small class, it is almost impossible for her to know you personally in a large lecture class. You should therefore make certain to see the professor at least once during office hours to introduce yourself. To help break the ice, try to come up with a specific question to ask about the class. During the course of your discussion, you can tell the professor a bit about yourself and your academic interests. Doing this ensures that the teacher has an impression of you as an individual, not as another face in the crowd.

CLASS PARTICIPATION

When class participation is part of the grade, many students make the mistake of thinking that they just need to talk a lot to get a good grade. However, there are many kinds of comments and questions, and some are much more intelligent and impressive than others.

Asking questions indicates a general interest in the class. However, students who constantly raise their hands and ask very basic questions about fairly obvious points can make a bad impression—they appear too lazy to make an effort to understand something for themselves. There is, however, a way to phrase a question that sounds more intelligent. For example, if you simply raise your hand and say, "I really don't get this. What does it all mean?" you sound like you just don't want to make the effort to understand the topic. However, if you say to a professor, "I see the point about Y and Z, but I'm having trouble understanding how they relate to X," you are asking a more specific question that reflects work to understand something. Try to make your questions very specific to indicate you have some knowledge and a genuine interest in clarifying a point.

Another way students earn credit for class participation is by making comments during class discussions. However, many students who feel compelled to say something in class will say whatever pops into their heads. If the comment re-states something that has already been said or merely points out something obvious, it won't impress the teacher; in fact, it can indicate you haven't been paying close attention. If you want to make a general comment, make certain it contributes something meaningful or makes a new point.

Not everyone is comfortable participating in class discussions or asking questions in front of large groups, and this doesn't necessarily detract from the class participation portion of a grade. If you are shy, visit the professor during office hours and discuss the course—this will demonstrate that you have an active interest in the class.

TAKE PRIDE IN YOUR WORK

Being a conscientious student means you take pride in your work; it indicates you are not just going through the motions of showing up for class, but are taking your work seriously.

The quality of the work you turn in indicates how conscientious you are. For example, an essay that has been carefully proofread and neatly typed shows you've put work into it and care about how it appears. However, an essay smudged with Liquid Paper and pencil marks, with spelling errors, and with a coffee stain on the cover page, sends the message that you really don't care all that much about the work. And the teacher will then not care all that much about reading it or the grade you get.

While there are specific things to do that show how conscientious you are, you also need to adopt a conscientious attitude. That way whatever you do, whether you are conscious of doing it to impress the teacher or not, will reflect well on you. Take pride in your work as a student, take your job seriously, and everything you do will reflect this positive attitude.

BEING AN EDUCATION CONSUMER

When you're a student, especially at a big school, it's easy to feel like a small part of a very large system. As you plow through miles of red tape and deal with headache-inducing bureaucracy, you can feel you have no control over your education, that your only option is to do what you are told.

Don't forget, though, that without students, there wouldn't be any education system. You are a vital part of any educational institution and, as such, you have a right to make as many demands on the system as it makes on you. Your education is at stake, and you have the right to get the best one possible—especially since you are paying for it.

If you read consumer magazines and advice guides, you'll see references to becoming an educated consumer. This means that before you make a major purchase, you do some research to get the best buy. You should similarly become an educated consumer of education. Get your money's worth from your school.

Being an educated consumer starts first with choosing a school that's right for you. There are, at the college level, thousands of universities out there, but only a handful are going to suit your interests and needs. Don't choose a school haphazardly based on what other people tell you or where you think you should go.

Do some research. Most schools are different than the glossy promotional brochures make them out to be. It's a good idea to visit them in person so you can see how things really are. The administrators and admissions office people will tell you one thing about a school, but students probably will tell you something else. Try to talk to students and ask about their perspectives. Do they like the school? Do they feel they are getting a good education?

Look carefully at recent statistics about the school. How many people drop out before graduating? How long does it take most students to get a degree? What percentage go on to find jobs within a year of graduating? What percentage go on to graduate or professional schools? If these statistics are poor, the school may not provide its students with everything it should.

Once you are attending a school, you should continue to think of yourself as an educated consumer. Most schools have a tremendous range of offerings; there are many different courses as well as many different teachers. However, both teachers and courses can range in quality. It would really be a shame to spend money for college credits and wind up in courses you just don't learn anything in. Sometimes a course won't be good because its content isn't something that interests you. More often than not, though, the deciding factor is the professor. A dynamic teacher can make the most mundane of subjects seem interesting. However, a poor teacher can make the most fascinating subject matter a total bore.

Before you select classes, do some research. First and foremost, think about whether the subject matter is interesting to you. Read the course description and find out if there is a sample syllabus available to look at—ask at the department office. Check out the reading list to see if it looks interesting. You can go to the bookstore to look over the books themselves.

To find out about a particular professor, ask around and talk to fellow students. Don't assume that just because a professor is famous or has won awards he is a good teacher; schools often hire big-name professors for their academic reputations, not for their teaching abilities. If you are thinking of taking a certain course, ask friends if they've ever had that particular professor and what they thought of him. You might even try sitting in on a professor's class to see what he is like.

If you are in high school, you probably don't have as much choice in determining what courses and teachers you have. However, you do have some opportunities to make decisions about what you study. For example, you'll usually have to choose a few elective courses each year. Whenever you do have some choice, be an educated consumer about it. Do some research about the course and the teacher before you sign up for anything.

Where Will I Go? Sources of Information About Colleges

If you are in high school and are beginning to look for a college, or if you are hoping to transfer to another college, there are many different sources of information you can consult. Because the following sources do not all provide the same kind of information, you should consult several of them. The more information you have, the more well-rounded the picture of the school you're researching will be.

College Guides. There are almost as many college guides on the market as there are colleges. Many guides simply list basic facts about the schools, such as the number of students, the student-to-teacher ratio, requirements to graduate, majors offered, and average SAT scores of those admitted; other guides are more subjective, trying to paint a portrait of life at the school and to elaborate on each school's strengths and weaknesses. Both kinds of books can be quite valuable, particularly in the early stages of your college search when you are identifying schools that are right for you. As you narrow down your choices, you can get more detailed information from other sources.

Web Sites. Many colleges and universities now have their own web sites on the Internet. If you have access, you can visit these sites and get a variety of information about a school. Check the World Wide Web yellow pages for listings. There are also several on-line college guides, many provided by the same publishers as the college guide books you see in the bookstore.

Information Directly from the Colleges. You can write to specific schools and request information. Keep in mind that their brochures are designed to present the school in the best possible light. Still, the brochure will provide important basic information. Additionally, try to get the course catalog to get an idea of the course offerings.

Speak to Friends and Relatives. Ask people where they went to school (or are currently going) and how they feel about it. Ask specific questions about assets and drawbacks. Keep in mind, though, that people are different. What one person may have loved or hated about the school may not affect you the same way. Be wary especially of the "Legacy Trap"—

Where Will I Go? Sources of Information About Colleges *(cont.)*

just because a close relative went to a particular school and loved it does not mean it's necessarily the best place for you. Consider your own interests and needs, and find a school that meets them.

Campus Visit. Visiting a school is an excellent way to get a tremendous amount of information about it. You'll see the campus the way it really looks, not as it appears in the glossy brochure photos. Go on a campus tour and check out the admissions office, where there is often some kind of information session for students. Make certain you talk to students; they will give you an accurate assessment of the school from the student's point of view. If possible, arrange to stay overnight in a dormitory (most schools make this experience available to applicants). Of course, visiting schools is time-consuming and can be expensive; you should plan to visit only those schools you are seriously considering attending.

FINDING A MENTOR

Your friends and family can offer you advice on many things, but a teacher is perhaps best qualified to offer specific advice about your education. For that reason, finding a faculty member who can serve as your mentor is extremely important. In addition to offering you advice, a mentor can help you negotiate the school's bureaucracy, discuss your future career or educational plans, write letters of recommendation, and much more.

Finding a mentor will take time and effort. There's no sign-up sheet for mentors, and no professor is going to knock on your door and volunteer. You need to find a professor who you like and respect, and then work to establish a relationship. At some point, you will take a course with a teacher who you really like. You can initially see this person during office hours, and on the first couple of visits simply discuss the course. If the professor seems receptive, you can eventually ask for advice on other aspects of your education and volunteer more information

about your own interests and goals. If you meet with the professor several times during the semester, you should begin to feel you are establishing a relationship. The key to finding a professor who becomes your mentor, though, is to maintain that relationship once the semester is over. Don't let a solid relationship with a teacher slip away. Make certain you continue meeting with the teacher, even if you are no longer taking her class.

MAKING THE MOST OF IT

Throughout this book, we've been emphasizing how important it is to be an active rather than a passive student. That not only applies to your specific study tasks, but to your entire attitude as a student. You can't sit back and place your education entirely in the hands of others. Teachers, books, and other educational resources can only do so much; ultimately, you must take control of your own education if it is going to have any value. In part, this means getting help when you need it. There are many resources available to help you when you are having difficulty, including caring teachers and tutoring programs, but you've got to make the effort to seek them out. At the same time, you can supplement your education on your own. Schools today are rich in resources and opportunities that can provide you with an exceptional, well-rounded education, from study-abroad programs and career internships to high-tech study centers and libraries. But these opportunities are not going to come knocking on your door; you need to take active measures to find and use them. If you make the most of your education, it will eventually mean much more to you than a diploma hanging on the wall.

In the meantime, good luck and happy studying.

Important Points to Remember

1. Develop productive study habits and make them a part of your daily routine. Change bad habits into good ones.

2. Treat being a student like a job; be professional, serious, and organized.

3. Set tasks for each day, week, and month.

4. Manage your time carefully; create a schedule that gives you flexibility each week to fulfill new tasks.

5. Make the right impression on your teacher. Take pride in your work.

6. Be an educated consumer.

7. Take control over your education and make the most of it.

INDEX

INDEX

vocabulary, 218, 249
    list, 250–251

W

web sites. See Internet
words, 163–164
    list of commonly misspelled, 154
    repeated, 97–98
    See also homophones; vocabulary

writing
    academic, 10, 68, 92, 96–99
    and reading, 249
    styles of, 161–162, 234
    See also essays

Notes

Notes

Notes

Notes

Notes

Notes